Editor
Mary S. Jones, M.A.

Editor in Chief
Karen J. Goldfluss, M.S. Ed.

Cover Artist
Barb Lorseyedi

Imaging
Leonard P. Swierski

Publisher
Mary D. Smith, M.S. Ed.

Practice Makes Perfect

TCR 8630

Fractions Decimals & Percents
GRADE 5

Includes practice for Standardized Tests

Teacher Created Resources

Author
Robert W. Smith

Teacher Created Resources, Inc.
6421 Industry Way
Westminster, CA 92683
www.teachercreated.com
ISBN: 978-1-4206-8630-2

© *2009 Teacher Created Resources, Inc.*
Made in U.S.A.

Teacher Created Resources

Table of Contents

Introduction

The old adage "practice makes perfect" can really hold true for your child and his or her education. The more practice and exposure your child has with concepts being taught in school, the more success he or she is likely to find. For many parents, knowing how to help your child can be frustrating because the resources may not be readily available and math textbooks can be more confusing than helpful. As a parent it is also difficult to know where to focus your efforts so that the extra practice your child receives at home supports what he or she is learning in school.

This book has been designed to help parents and teachers reinforce basic skills with their children. *Practice Makes Perfect* reviews basic math skills in grade 5. The math focus is on fractions, decimals, and percents. These interrelated concepts are often difficult for even very capable students to grasp. While it would be impossible to include all math concepts taught in grade 5 in this book, the following basic objectives are reinforced through practice exercises arranged in a logical, sequential, and easy-to-use format. These objectives support math standards established on a district, state, or national level. (Refer to the Table of Contents for the specific objectives of each practice page.)

- Equivalent fractions
- Adding, subtracting, multiplying, and dividing fractions and decimals
- Converting fractions, decimals, and percents
- Working with mixed numbers and improper fractions
- Computing common denominators

- Reducing fractions
- Comparing and ordering fractions and decimals
- Computing percents
- Operations with money
- Computing simple interest

There are 36 practice pages organized sequentially, so children can build their knowledge from more basic skills to higher-level math skills. (NOTE: Have children show all of their work where computation is necessary to solve a problem.) Following the practice pages are six practice tests. These provide children with multiple-choice test items to help prepare them for standardized tests administered in schools. You may use the fill-in answer sheet on page 46. To correct the test pages and practice pages in this book, use the answer key provided on pages 47 and 48.

How to Make the Most of This Book

Here are some useful ideas for optimizing the practice pages in this book:

- Set aside a specific place in your home to work on the practice pages. Keep it neat and tidy with materials on hand.
- Set up a certain time of day to work on the practice pages. This will establish consistency. An alternative is to look for times in your day or week that are less hectic and are more conducive to practicing skills.
- Keep all practice sessions with your child positive and constructive.
- Help with instructions if necessary. If your child is having difficulty understanding what to do or how to get started, work through the first problem with him or her.
- Review the work your child has done. This serves as reinforcement and provides further practice.
- Allow your child to use whatever writing instruments he or she prefers. For example, colored pencils can add variety and pleasure to drill work.
- Pay attention to the areas in which your child has the most difficulty. Provide extra guidance and exercises in those areas. Allowing children to use drawings and manipulatives, such as coins, tiles, game markers, or flash cards can help them grasp difficult concepts more easily.
- Look for ways to make real-life applications to the skills being reinforced.

Practice 1

Reminder

A fraction is a part of a whole. In the shape below, one of the four parts of the square is shaded. So $\frac{1}{4}$ of the square is represented.

$= \frac{1}{4}$ ← numerator (parts you are talking about)
   ← denominator (total parts in a whole)

Directions: Write the fraction representing the shaded portion of each shape. Write your answer next to each shape.

1.
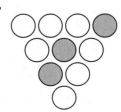

2.

3.

4.
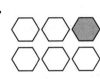

5.

6.

7.

8.

9.
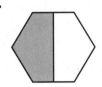

10.

11.

12.
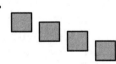

13.

14.

15.

16.

17.

18.
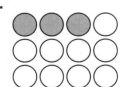

19.

20.

21.
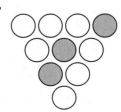

22.

23.

24.
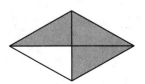

Practice 2

Reminder

- Equivalent fractions describe the same amount or the same area, but they are expressed in a different number of pieces or parts.
- Equivalent fractions are equal to each other.

$$\frac{1}{2} = \frac{2}{4} = \frac{4}{8} = \frac{8}{16}$$

- You can create equivalent fractions by multiplying or dividing the numerator and the denominator by the same number.

$$\frac{3 \times 2 = 6}{4 \times 2 = 8} \quad \text{so} \quad \frac{3}{4} = \frac{6}{8} \qquad \frac{12 \div 3 = 4}{24 \div 3 = 8} \quad \text{so} \quad \frac{12}{24} = \frac{4}{8}$$

Directions: Write the equivalent fraction for each given fraction below. The first two are done for you.

1. $\frac{1}{2} = \frac{2}{4}$

2. $\frac{4}{6} = \frac{2}{3}$

3. $\frac{1}{8} = \frac{2}{\quad}$

4. $\frac{3}{4} = \frac{\quad}{8}$

5. $\frac{4}{5} = \frac{\quad}{10}$

6. $\frac{3}{5} = \frac{\quad}{10}$

7. $\frac{3}{9} = \frac{\quad}{3}$

8. $\frac{9}{12} = \frac{\quad}{4}$

9. $\frac{3}{8} = \frac{\quad}{16}$

10. $\frac{6}{12} = \frac{\quad}{2}$

11. $\frac{10}{12} = \frac{\quad}{6}$

12. $\frac{5}{10} = \frac{\quad}{2}$

13. $\frac{4}{4} = \frac{\quad}{12}$

14. $\frac{7}{8} = \frac{\quad}{24}$

15. $\frac{5}{9} = \frac{\quad}{18}$

16. $\frac{2}{2} = \frac{\quad}{6}$

17. $\frac{3}{3} = \frac{\quad}{12}$

18. $\frac{4}{4} = \frac{\quad}{20}$

Directions: Multiply to compute these equivalent fractions. The first one is done for you.

19. $\frac{2}{7} \times \frac{2}{2} = \frac{4}{14}$

20. $\frac{4}{5} \times \frac{4}{4} =$

21. $\frac{3}{12} \times \frac{2}{2} =$

22. $\frac{1}{3} \times \frac{3}{3} =$

23. $\frac{1}{4} \times \frac{2}{2} =$

24. $\frac{2}{6} \times \frac{4}{4} =$

25. $\frac{4}{5} \times \frac{3}{3} =$

26. $\frac{1}{3} \times \frac{8}{8} =$

27. $\frac{4}{9} \times \frac{2}{2} =$

Practice 3

Reminder

- Fractions are in their lowest terms when no factor greater than 1 will divide evenly into both the numerator and the denominator.

  Examples: $\frac{2}{5}, \frac{7}{10}, \frac{2}{7}, \frac{3}{8}$

- All fractions with 1 as the numerator and all fractions where the numerator is 1 less than the denominator are in lowest terms.

  Examples: $\frac{1}{2}, \frac{1}{3}, \frac{3}{4}, \frac{7}{8}$

- To reduce fractions, find the **greatest common factor** (GCF). Divide the numerator and the denominator by the greatest common factor. Reduce $\frac{12}{16}$, GCF of 12 and 16 is 4.

  factors of 12: 1, 2, 3, 4, 6, 12 $\frac{12 \div 4 = 3}{16 \div 4 = 4}$ so $\frac{12}{16} = \frac{3}{4}$
  factors of 16: 1, 2, 4, 8, 16

Directions: Find the greatest common factor and reduce each fraction to lowest terms. The first two are done for you.

1. $\frac{4}{6} = \frac{\div 2}{\div 2} = \frac{2}{3}$ 2. $\frac{5}{10} = \frac{\div 5}{\div 5} = \frac{1}{2}$ 3. $\frac{7}{21} =$ 4. $\frac{14}{16} =$

   GCF = 2   GCF = 5   GCF =   GCF =

5. $\frac{5}{15} =$ 6. $\frac{2}{8} =$ 7. $\frac{12}{24} =$ 8. $\frac{5}{25} =$

   GCF =   GCF =   GCF =   GCF =

9. $\frac{6}{9} =$ 10. $\frac{7}{14} =$ 11. $\frac{25}{50} =$ 12. $\frac{15}{25} =$

   GCF =   GCF =   GCF =   GCF =

13. $\frac{9}{18} =$ 14. $\frac{9}{15} =$ 15. $\frac{22}{33} =$ 16. $\frac{14}{21} =$

   GCF =   GCF =   GCF =   GCF =

17. $\frac{12}{18} =$ 18. $\frac{20}{24} =$ 19. $\frac{27}{33} =$ 20. $\frac{30}{36} =$

   GCF =   GCF =   GCF =   GCF =

21. $\frac{40}{50} =$ 22. $\frac{18}{24} =$ 23. $\frac{16}{24} =$ 24. $\frac{18}{27} =$

   GCF =   GCF =   GCF =   GCF =

Practice 4

Reminder

- Improper fractions have a numerator equal to or larger than the denominator. They have a value of 1 or greater.

  Examples: $\frac{3}{2}, \frac{5}{5}, \frac{8}{3}, \frac{9}{2}$

- Mixed numbers contain a whole number and a fraction. They have a value greater than 1.

  Examples: $3\frac{1}{2}, 4\frac{2}{3}, 5\frac{1}{5}, 7\frac{4}{5}, 4\frac{3}{4}$

- Mixed numbers are created from improper fractions by dividing the numerator by the denominator.

  Examples: $\frac{5}{2} = 5 \div 2 = 2\frac{1}{2}$ $\frac{7}{3} = 7 \div 3 = 2\frac{1}{3}$ $\frac{4}{3} = 4 \div 3 = 1\frac{1}{3}$

- Mixed numbers are converted into improper fractions by multiplying the denominator times the whole number and adding the numerator. This number becomes the numerator in the improper fraction. The denominator in the improper fraction is the same denominator that you started with in the mixed number.

  Examples: $2\frac{1}{3} = (3 \times 2) + 1 = \frac{7}{3}$ $5\frac{3}{4} = (4 \times 5) + 3 = \frac{23}{4}$

Directions: Change these improper fractions into mixed numbers. The first two are done for you.

1. $\frac{3}{2} = 3 \div 2 = 1\frac{1}{2}$ 2. $\frac{5}{4} = 5 \div 4 = 1\frac{1}{4}$ 3. $\frac{6}{5} =$

4. $\frac{7}{6} =$ 5. $\frac{9}{4} =$ 6. $\frac{9}{5} =$

7. $\frac{19}{10} =$ 8. $\frac{12}{7} =$ 9. $\frac{17}{6} =$

Directions: Change these improper fractions to whole numbers. The first one is done for you.

10. $\frac{9}{3} = 9 \div 3 = 3$ 11. $\frac{8}{2} =$ 12. $\frac{12}{4} =$

13. $\frac{16}{8} =$ 14. $\frac{25}{5} =$ 15. $\frac{20}{5} =$

Directions: Change these mixed numbers to improper fractions. The first one is done for you.

16. $3\frac{2}{3} = (3 \times 3) + 2 = \frac{11}{3}$ 17. $4\frac{2}{3} =$ 18. $6\frac{1}{2} =$

19. $5\frac{1}{2} =$ 20. $2\frac{1}{4} =$ 21. $4\frac{1}{5} =$

22. $3\frac{1}{3} =$ 23. $2\frac{3}{4} =$ 24. $7\frac{1}{3} =$

25. $4\frac{1}{2} =$ 26. $2\frac{1}{6} =$ 27. $5\frac{1}{2} =$

28. $4\frac{3}{4} =$ 29. $3\frac{3}{4} =$ 30. $1\frac{1}{12} =$

Practice 5 ✺ ૭ ৬ ✺ ✺ ৬ ✺ ૭ ✺ ૭ ✺

Reminder

To compare fractions with unlike denominators, you first need to compute the common denominator by finding the **least common multiple** (LCM) of the two denominators.

To get the lowest common denominator for $\frac{1}{3}$ and $\frac{3}{4}$, find the LCM of 3 and 4.

- multiples of 3: 3, 6, 9, ⑫, 15 . . .
- multiples of 4: 4, 8, ⑫, 16 . . .   ⟶ 12 is the LCM

Multiply the numerator by the same number you multiplied the denominator in order to get the LCM.

Now compare the numerators. 4 is less than 6, so $\frac{4}{12}$ is less than $\frac{6}{12}$. That means $\frac{1}{3}$ is less than $\frac{2}{4}$.

$$\frac{1}{3} \times \frac{4}{4} = \frac{4}{12} \qquad\qquad \frac{2}{4} \times \frac{3}{3} = \frac{6}{12}$$

Directions: Use > (greater than), < (less than), or = (equal to) to compare each set of fractions below after computing the lowest common denominator. The first two are done for you.

1. $\frac{1}{2}$ __< __ $\frac{2}{3}$

$\frac{1}{2} \times \frac{3}{3} = \frac{3}{6}$

$\frac{2}{3} \times \frac{2}{2} = \frac{4}{6}$

2. $\frac{2}{4}$ __< __ $\frac{3}{5}$

$\frac{2}{4} \times \frac{5}{5} = \frac{10}{20}$

$\frac{3}{5} \times \frac{4}{4} = \frac{12}{20}$

3. $\frac{3}{8}$ _____ $\frac{2}{3}$

4. $\frac{2}{4}$ _____ $\frac{7}{8}$

5. $\frac{5}{6}$ _____ $\frac{2}{3}$

6. $\frac{4}{8}$ _____ $\frac{1}{7}$

7. $\frac{2}{5}$ _____ $\frac{1}{2}$

8. $\frac{5}{9}$ _____ $\frac{1}{2}$

9. $\frac{4}{7}$ _____ $\frac{1}{3}$

10. $\frac{2}{7}$ _____ $\frac{3}{8}$

11. $\frac{1}{3}$ _____ $\frac{4}{9}$

12. $\frac{4}{8}$ _____ $\frac{3}{5}$

13. $\frac{3}{10}$ _____ $\frac{1}{3}$

14. $\frac{2}{3}$ _____ $\frac{3}{4}$

15. $\frac{3}{4}$ _____ $\frac{4}{6}$

16. $\frac{4}{5}$ _____ $\frac{3}{4}$

17. $\frac{5}{6}$ _____ $\frac{3}{5}$

18. $\frac{2}{8}$ _____ $\frac{1}{3}$

Practice 6

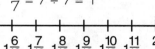
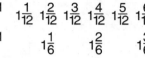

Reminder

Improper fractions can be converted to mixed numbers before comparing fractions and mixed numbers.

$$\frac{3}{2} = 3 \div 2 = 1\frac{1}{2} \qquad \frac{5}{4} = 5 \div 4 = 1\frac{1}{4} \qquad \frac{7}{7} = 7 \div 7 = 1$$

[number line diagram showing fractions from 0 to 2 with twelfths, sixths, fourths, thirds, and halves marked]

Directions: Use < (less than), > (greater than), or = (equal to) to compare these fractions and mixed numbers. The first two are done for you.

1. $\frac{3}{2}$ ___>___ $1\frac{1}{4}$

   $1\frac{1}{2} > 1\frac{1}{4}$

2. $\frac{6}{5}$ ___=___ $1\frac{1}{5}$

   $1\frac{1}{5} = 1\frac{1}{5}$

3. $\frac{5}{4}$ _____ $1\frac{3}{4}$

4. $\frac{9}{8}$ _____ $2\frac{1}{8}$

5. $\frac{3}{2}$ _____ $1\frac{1}{3}$

6. $\frac{5}{3}$ _____ $\frac{3}{2}$

7. $1\frac{1}{3}$ _____ $\frac{8}{6}$

8. $\frac{7}{4}$ _____ $1\frac{1}{2}$

9. $1\frac{1}{3}$ _____ $\frac{7}{3}$

10. $1\frac{7}{8}$ _____ $\frac{8}{4}$

11. $1\frac{1}{2}$ _____ $\frac{6}{4}$

12. $\frac{5}{4}$ _____ $1\frac{2}{3}$

13. $\frac{7}{12}$ _____ $\frac{3}{4}$

14. $\frac{5}{3}$ _____ $1\frac{6}{12}$

15. $1\frac{1}{12}$ _____ $1\frac{1}{4}$

16. $1\frac{7}{12}$ _____ $\frac{6}{4}$

17. $\frac{10}{6}$ _____ $\frac{19}{12}$

18. $1\frac{5}{6}$ _____ $1\frac{3}{4}$

19. $\frac{4}{3}$ _____ $\frac{6}{4}$

20. $\frac{9}{6}$ _____ $1\frac{1}{3}$

21. $1\frac{3}{4}$ _____ $\frac{5}{3}$

22. $1\frac{1}{2}$ _____ $\frac{7}{4}$

23. $\frac{11}{8}$ _____ $1\frac{1}{2}$

24. $\frac{8}{4}$ _____ $1\frac{4}{6}$

Practice 7

Reminder

- Fractions can be converted to common denominators to help place them in the correct order.

  Example: Put $\frac{3}{4}$, $\frac{1}{2}$, $\frac{2}{3}$ in order from least to greatest. Lowest common denominator is 12.

  $\frac{3}{4} = \frac{9}{12}$ $\qquad$ $\frac{1}{2} = \frac{6}{12}$ $\qquad$ $\frac{2}{3} = \frac{8}{12}$ $\qquad$ so the correct order is $\frac{1}{2}, \frac{2}{3}, \frac{3}{4}$

- Improper fractions can be converted to mixed numbers before ordering fractions and mixed numbers.

  $\frac{5}{2} = 2\frac{1}{2}$ $\qquad$ $\frac{7}{4} = 1\frac{3}{4}$ $\qquad$ $\frac{12}{6} = 2$ $\qquad$ so the correct order is $\frac{7}{4}, \frac{12}{6}, \frac{5}{2}$

Directions: Use common denominators to place these fractions and mixed numbers in order from **least to greatest**. The first two are done for you.

1. $\frac{3}{4}$ _____ $\frac{5}{8}$
   $\frac{5}{8}$ _____ $\frac{3}{4}$
   $1\frac{1}{2}$ _____ $1\frac{1}{2}$

2. $\frac{4}{12}$ _____ $\frac{4}{12}$
   $1\frac{3}{6}$ _____ $1\frac{1}{3}$
   $1\frac{1}{3}$ _____ $1\frac{3}{6}$

3. $\frac{3}{9}$ _____
   $\frac{1}{2}$ _____
   $\frac{4}{3}$ _____

4. $\frac{9}{8}$ _____
   $1\frac{3}{4}$ _____
   $\frac{5}{6}$ _____

5. $\frac{4}{6}$ _____
   $2\frac{1}{2}$ _____
   $\frac{9}{8}$ _____

6. $\frac{3}{12}$ _____
   $1\frac{7}{8}$ _____
   $\frac{4}{3}$ _____

7. $\frac{5}{12}$ _____
   $\frac{7}{5}$ _____
   $\frac{7}{8}$ _____

8. $\frac{3}{4}$ _____
   $\frac{5}{6}$ _____
   $\frac{11}{6}$ _____

9. $\frac{3}{2}$ _____
   $\frac{7}{8}$ _____
   $2\frac{1}{4}$ _____

10. $\frac{3}{9}$ _____
    $\frac{6}{3}$ _____
    $\frac{1}{2}$ _____

11. $\frac{9}{10}$ _____
    $1\frac{1}{2}$ _____
    $\frac{1}{4}$ _____

12. $3\frac{1}{2}$ _____
    $\frac{4}{3}$ _____
    $\frac{3}{4}$ _____

13. $\frac{2}{1}$ _____
    $\frac{1}{2}$ _____
    $\frac{5}{8}$ _____

14. $\frac{4}{2}$ _____
    $2\frac{1}{2}$ _____
    $\frac{3}{4}$ _____

15. $\frac{7}{12}$ _____
    $\frac{5}{3}$ _____
    $\frac{3}{6}$ _____

16. $\frac{6}{4}$ _____
    $1\frac{3}{4}$ _____
    $\frac{6}{12}$ _____

17. $\frac{4}{6}$ _____
    $\frac{3}{2}$ _____
    $1\frac{1}{3}$ _____

18. $\frac{9}{3}$ _____
    $1\frac{2}{3}$ _____
    $\frac{4}{12}$ _____

19. $\frac{1}{6}$ _____
    $\frac{6}{2}$ _____
    $2\frac{1}{3}$ _____

20. $\frac{3}{2}$ _____
    $\frac{2}{1}$ _____
    $1\frac{5}{8}$ _____

21. $\frac{12}{6}$ _____
    $1\frac{7}{8}$ _____
    $\frac{7}{4}$ _____

22. $\frac{8}{6}$ _____
    $1\frac{4}{8}$ _____
    $\frac{3}{4}$ _____

23. $3\frac{1}{4}$ _____
    $\frac{9}{4}$ _____
    $\frac{2}{3}$ _____

24. $\frac{7}{2}$ _____
    $2\frac{1}{3}$ _____
    $\frac{10}{12}$ _____

Practice 8

Reminder

- The **lowest common denominator** (LCD) is the smallest number both denominators will divide into evenly. This is called the **least common multiple** (LCM).
- The LCD is never smaller than the larger of the two denominators.
- Always try the larger denominator to see if both denominators will divide evenly into it.
- Multiply the larger denominator by 2 and see if both denominators will divide into it. If not, multiply by 3 or 4.
- If the denominators are prime numbers or next to each other in counting order, multiply them to find the LCD.

Examples: $\frac{1}{4}$ and $\frac{1}{6}$ (Multiply 6 x 2 = 12) $\frac{1}{3}$ and $\frac{1}{4}$ (Multiply 4 x 3 = 12)
12 is the LCD   12 is the LCD

Directions: Find the LCD/LCM for these pairs of fractions. The first two are done for you.

1. $\frac{2}{5}$ and $\frac{2}{3}$
   LCD = _____15_____

2. $\frac{4}{8}$ and $\frac{1}{6}$
   LCD = _____24_____

3. $\frac{3}{4}$ and $\frac{1}{3}$
   LCD = _____

4. $\frac{5}{12}$ and $\frac{1}{4}$
   LCD = _____

5. $\frac{1}{6}$ and $\frac{2}{5}$
   LCD = _____

6. $\frac{1}{2}$ and $\frac{3}{7}$
   LCD = _____

7. $\frac{5}{12}$ and $\frac{3}{8}$
   LCD = _____

8. $\frac{2}{3}$ and $\frac{1}{6}$
   LCD = _____

9. $\frac{4}{8}$ and $\frac{2}{4}$
   LCD = _____

10. $\frac{3}{9}$ and $\frac{1}{3}$
    LCD = _____

11. $\frac{4}{9}$ and $\frac{2}{6}$
    LCD = _____

12. $\frac{3}{8}$ and $\frac{2}{10}$
    LCD = _____

13. $\frac{3}{10}$ and $\frac{1}{2}$
    LCD = _____

14. $\frac{5}{10}$ and $\frac{3}{12}$
    LCD = _____

15. $\frac{3}{9}$ and $\frac{3}{12}$
    LCD = _____

16. $\frac{2}{9}$ and $\frac{5}{6}$
    LCD = _____

17. $\frac{7}{8}$ and $\frac{4}{5}$
    LCD = _____

18. $\frac{1}{21}$ and $\frac{5}{7}$
    LCD = _____

19. $\frac{3}{15}$ and $\frac{2}{10}$
    LCD = _____

20. $\frac{5}{16}$ and $\frac{2}{4}$
    LCD = _____

21. $\frac{3}{9}$ and $\frac{3}{27}$
    LCD = _____

Practice 9

Reminder

- When adding and subtracting fractions with common denominators, add or subtract the numerators and keep the denominator the same.

$$\frac{1}{3} + \frac{1}{3} = \frac{2}{3} \qquad \frac{4}{5} - \frac{1}{5} = \frac{3}{5}$$

- When adding and subtracting fractions with unlike denominators, determine the lowest common denominator and then add or subtract.

$$\begin{array}{r} \frac{3}{4} = \frac{3}{4} \\ -\frac{1}{2} = \frac{2}{4} \\ \hline \frac{1}{4} \end{array}$$

- Reduce all answers to lowest terms.

Directions: Add or subtract these fractions. Reduce answers to lowest terms. Three examples are done for you.

1. $\frac{1}{4} + \frac{2}{4} = \frac{3}{4}$

2. $\frac{5}{8} - \frac{3}{8} = \frac{2}{8} = \frac{1}{4}$

3. $\frac{5}{6} - \frac{2}{6} =$

4. $\frac{5}{8} - \frac{4}{8} =$

5. $\frac{9}{10} - \frac{4}{10} =$

6. $\frac{4}{9} + \frac{2}{9} =$

7. $\begin{array}{r} \frac{2}{10} = \frac{4}{20} \\ +\ \frac{3}{4} = \frac{15}{20} \\ \hline \frac{19}{20} \end{array}$

8. $\begin{array}{r} \frac{1}{12} \\ +\ \frac{4}{6} \\ \hline \end{array}$

9. $\begin{array}{r} \frac{3}{10} \\ +\ \frac{2}{5} \\ \hline \end{array}$

10. $\begin{array}{r} \frac{4}{5} \\ -\ \frac{12}{20} \\ \hline \end{array}$

11. $\begin{array}{r} \frac{2}{8} \\ +\ \frac{4}{12} \\ \hline \end{array}$

12. $\begin{array}{r} \frac{3}{8} \\ -\ \frac{1}{6} \\ \hline \end{array}$

13. $\begin{array}{r} \frac{13}{15} \\ -\ \frac{3}{5} \\ \hline \end{array}$

14. $\begin{array}{r} \frac{6}{11} \\ +\ \frac{2}{3} \\ \hline \end{array}$

15. $\begin{array}{r} \frac{3}{6} \\ -\ \frac{1}{8} \\ \hline \end{array}$

16. $\begin{array}{r} \frac{1}{4} \\ +\ \frac{1}{9} \\ \hline \end{array}$

17. $\begin{array}{r} \frac{8}{12} \\ +\ \frac{2}{3} \\ \hline \end{array}$

18. $\begin{array}{r} \frac{5}{6} \\ -\ \frac{4}{12} \\ \hline \end{array}$

19. $\begin{array}{r} \frac{7}{10} \\ -\ \frac{3}{5} \\ \hline \end{array}$

20. $\begin{array}{r} \frac{5}{9} \\ -\ \frac{1}{6} \\ \hline \end{array}$

21. $\begin{array}{r} \frac{11}{18} \\ -\ \frac{1}{12} \\ \hline \end{array}$

22. $\begin{array}{r} \frac{10}{12} \\ +\ \frac{2}{8} \\ \hline \end{array}$

23. $\begin{array}{r} \frac{3}{5} \\ +\ \frac{2}{7} \\ \hline \end{array}$

24. $\begin{array}{r} \frac{13}{20} \\ -\ \frac{4}{8} \\ \hline \end{array}$

25. $\begin{array}{r} \frac{3}{4} \\ -\ \frac{5}{8} \\ \hline \end{array}$

26. $\begin{array}{r} \frac{2}{15} \\ +\ \frac{1}{3} \\ \hline \end{array}$

Practice 10 ❧ ⟲ ❧ ❧ ⟲ ❧ ⟲ ❧ ⟲ ❧

Reminder

- Before adding or subtracting fractions or mixed numbers, compute the lowest common denominator.
- Convert all fractions to equivalent fractions in that denominator.
- Add or subtract the fractions.
- Add or subtract the whole numbers.

Example:

$$2\frac{1}{2} = 2\frac{2}{4}$$
$$-1\frac{1}{4} = -1\frac{1}{4}$$
$$\overline{1\frac{1}{4}}$$

Directions: Add or subtract the fractions and mixed numbers following the steps above. The first two are done for you.

1. $\quad 3\frac{2}{3} = \quad 3\frac{8}{12}$
$\quad -2\frac{1}{4} = \quad -2\frac{3}{12}$
$\quad\quad\quad\quad\quad\quad 1\frac{5}{12}$

2. $\quad 4\frac{5}{8} = \quad 4\frac{15}{24}$
$\quad +2\frac{1}{3} = \quad +2\frac{8}{24}$
$\quad\quad\quad\quad\quad\quad 6\frac{23}{24}$

3. $\quad 3\frac{1}{3}$
$\quad +2\frac{1}{2}$

4. $\quad 5\frac{4}{5}$
$\quad -2\frac{1}{10}$

5. $\quad 3\frac{1}{4}$
$\quad +3\frac{1}{2}$

6. $\quad 9\frac{4}{9}$
$\quad -5\frac{1}{3}$

7. $\quad 6\frac{7}{8}$
$\quad -2\frac{3}{4}$

8. $\quad 7\frac{1}{2}$
$\quad -2\frac{1}{8}$

9. $\quad 6\frac{3}{8}$
$\quad +2\frac{1}{3}$

10. $\quad 5\frac{1}{2}$
$\quad -\frac{3}{8}$

11. $\quad 4\frac{1}{7}$
$\quad +\frac{1}{4}$

12. $\quad 3\frac{1}{6}$
$\quad +\frac{2}{3}$

13. $\quad 5\frac{4}{6}$
$\quad -\frac{1}{4}$

14. $\quad 6\frac{1}{12}$
$\quad +\frac{1}{3}$

15. $\quad 9\frac{1}{2}$
$\quad +\frac{1}{3}$

16. $\quad 3\frac{1}{6}$
$\quad +1\frac{2}{3}$

17. $\quad 1\frac{1}{10}$
$\quad +1\frac{1}{5}$

18. $\quad 3\frac{1}{8}$
$\quad +2\frac{1}{4}$

Practice 11

Reminder

- When adding the fractional part of a mixed number, you may have a fraction with a value greater than 1. Convert this improper fraction to a whole number and fraction. Add the new whole number to the whole number from your original answer.

$$\text{Example:} \quad 2\frac{3}{4} = 2\frac{9}{12} \qquad\qquad \frac{17}{12} = 17 \div 12 = 1\frac{5}{12}$$

$$+\; 3\frac{2}{3} = 3\frac{8}{12}$$

$$5\frac{17}{12} = 5 + 1\frac{5}{12} = 6\frac{5}{12}$$

- When subtracting the fractional part of a mixed number, you may be subtracting a fraction with a greater value from one of lesser value. Regroup by borrowing 1 from the whole number and converting it to a fraction with the common denominator you are using.

$$\text{Example:} \quad 4\frac{1}{3} = 4\frac{2}{6} = 3\frac{6}{6} + \frac{2}{6} = \quad 3\frac{8}{6}$$

$$-\; 2\frac{5}{6} = 2\frac{5}{6} \qquad\qquad\qquad\qquad -\; 2\frac{5}{6}$$

$$1\frac{3}{6} = 1\frac{1}{12}$$

Directions: Complete these addition problems. Regroup where necessary. Reduce answers to lowest terms. The first one is done for you.

1. $3\frac{2}{3} = 3\frac{4}{6}$

    $+\; 2\frac{1}{2} = 2\frac{3}{6}$

    $5\frac{7}{6} = 6\frac{1}{6}$

2. $3\frac{1}{2}$

    $+\; 2\frac{5}{8}$

3. $6\frac{1}{4}$

    $+\; 3\frac{9}{12}$

4. $5\frac{1}{3}$

    $+\; 1\frac{5}{6}$

5. $4\frac{3}{5}$

    $+\; 1\frac{1}{2}$

6. $2\frac{1}{2}$

    $+\; 1\frac{3}{4}$

7. $4\frac{8}{9}$

    $+\; 2\frac{2}{3}$

8. $3\frac{2}{3}$

    $+\; 6\frac{3}{4}$

Directions: Complete these subtraction problems. Regroup where necessary. Reduce answers to lowest terms. The first one is done for you. Use another sheet of paper to show your work.

9. $4\frac{1}{3} = 3\frac{8}{6}$

    $-\; 1\frac{3}{6} = 1\frac{3}{6}$

    $2\frac{5}{6}$

10. $6\frac{1}{2}$

    $-\; 2\frac{3}{4}$

11. $4\frac{1}{8}$

    $-\; 1\frac{1}{3}$

12. $5\frac{1}{3}$

    $-\; 2\frac{5}{6}$

13. $4\frac{1}{5}$

    $-\; 1\frac{1}{3}$

14. $2\frac{1}{4}$

    $-\; 1\frac{11}{12}$

15. $2\frac{1}{6}$

    $-\; 1\frac{3}{4}$

16. $7\frac{5}{6}$

    $-\; 2\frac{1}{4}$

Practice 12 🐚 🌀 🐚 🌀 🐚 🌀 🐚 🌀 🐚 🌀

Reminder

- When you multiply a fraction times a whole number, multiply the whole number times the numerator and divide the answer by the denominator.

  Example: $3 \times \frac{4}{5} = 3 \times 4 = \frac{12}{5} = 2\frac{2}{5}$

- "of" means multiply: $\frac{1}{3}$ of $6 = \frac{1}{3} \times 6 = 1 \times 6 = \frac{6}{3} = 2$

Directions: Multiply the fractions times the whole numbers in these problems. Reduce all answers to lowest terms. The first two are done for you.

1. $3 \times \frac{3}{8} =$

$3 \times 3 = \frac{9}{8} = 1\frac{1}{8}$

2. $\frac{4}{9} \times 12 =$

$4 \times 12 = \frac{48}{9} =$

$5\frac{3}{9} = 5\frac{1}{3}$

3. $4 \times \frac{1}{2} =$

4. $5 \times \frac{3}{7} =$

5. $3 \times \frac{4}{5} =$

6. $\frac{5}{6} \times 2 =$

7. $\frac{4}{5} \times 20 =$

8. $6 \times \frac{7}{12} =$

9. $\frac{3}{8} \times 5 =$

10. $\frac{3}{4} \times 12 =$

11. $5 \times \frac{1}{4} =$

12. $20 \times \frac{3}{4} =$

13. $\frac{3}{11} \times 33 =$

14. $7 \times \frac{3}{10} =$

15. $12 \times \frac{5}{8} =$

16. $\frac{1}{9} \times 18 =$

17. $22 \times \frac{5}{11} =$

18. $\frac{6}{8} \times 16 =$

19. $\frac{1}{5}$ of $10 =$

20. $\frac{1}{2}$ of $6 =$

21. $\frac{3}{8}$ of $24 =$

22. $\frac{4}{9}$ of $36 =$

23. $\frac{1}{3}$ of $18 =$

24. $\frac{5}{6}$ of $24 =$

25. $\frac{1}{3}$ of $21 =$

26. $\frac{2}{3}$ of $15 =$

27. $\frac{2}{3}$ of $9 =$

28. $\frac{3}{4}$ of $5 =$

Practice 13 ✺ ꙿ ꙿ ✺ ✺ ꙿ ✺ ꙿ ✺ ꙿ ✺

Reminder
1. Cross cancel before you multiply fractions if you can. This will save you from having to reduce your answer later.
2. Look for any numerator greater than 1 that fits evenly into any denominator.
3. Look for any denominator greater than 1 that fits evenly into any numerator.
4. Look for any number greater than 1 that fits into numbers on the top and bottom.

Examples: $\frac{2}{3} \times \frac{1}{5} = \frac{2}{15}$ $\frac{^1\cancel{3}}{_2\cancel{8}} \times \frac{\cancel{4}^1}{\cancel{9}_3} = \frac{1}{6}$

(no cross canceling needed)

Directions: Multiply these fractions. Cross cancel if you can. The first two are done for you.

1. $\frac{^1\cancel{2}}{3} \times \frac{1}{\cancel{2}_1} = \frac{1}{3}$ 2. $\frac{^1\cancel{4}}{_1\cancel{5}} \times \frac{\cancel{15}^3}{\cancel{20}_5} = \frac{3}{5}$ 3. $\frac{1}{7} \times \frac{21}{4} =$ 4. $\frac{2}{9} \times \frac{3}{4} =$

5. $\frac{6}{8} \times \frac{2}{3} =$ 6. $\frac{2}{5} \times \frac{10}{12} =$ 7. $\frac{3}{7} \times \frac{14}{15} =$ 8. $\frac{1}{4} \times \frac{8}{5} =$

9. $\frac{3}{4} \times \frac{8}{15} =$ 10. $\frac{4}{12} \times \frac{5}{15} =$ 11. $\frac{3}{8} \times \frac{8}{9} =$ 12. $\frac{15}{5} \times \frac{4}{8} =$

13. $\frac{7}{13} \times \frac{1}{7} =$ 14. $\frac{5}{8} \times \frac{2}{10} =$ 15. $\frac{15}{25} \times \frac{5}{3} =$ 16. $\frac{1}{3} \times \frac{6}{7} =$

17. $\frac{3}{5} \times \frac{2}{7} =$ 18. $\frac{4}{11} \times \frac{33}{44} =$ 19. $\frac{4}{6} \times \frac{10}{15} =$ 20. $\frac{14}{20} \times \frac{9}{21} =$

21. $\frac{6}{16} \times \frac{9}{15} =$ 22. $\frac{12}{14} \times \frac{6}{10} =$ 23. $\frac{3}{15} \times \frac{4}{16} =$ 24. $\frac{6}{8} \times \frac{2}{4} =$

Practice 14

Reminder

To divide two fractions: $\frac{3}{4} \div \frac{1}{4} =$

1. Get the reciprocal of the second fraction by inverting the fraction (turning it upside down). $\frac{1}{4}$ becomes $\frac{4}{1}$.
2. Change the sign to multiplication (x).
3. Multiply the fractions.
4. Reduce the answer to lowest terms.

$$\frac{3}{4} \div \frac{1}{4} =$$
$$\frac{3}{4} \times \frac{4}{1} = \frac{12}{4} = 3$$

Directions: Divide these fractions. Reduce to lowest terms. The first two are done for you.

1. $\frac{2}{3} \div \frac{1}{2} =$

   $\frac{2}{3} \times \frac{2}{1} = \frac{4}{3} = 1\frac{1}{3}$

2. $\frac{3}{4} \div \frac{1}{3} =$

   $\frac{3}{4} \times \frac{3}{1} = \frac{9}{4} = 2\frac{1}{4}$

3. $\frac{4}{5} \div \frac{2}{3} =$

4. $\frac{4}{5} \div \frac{1}{5} =$

5. $\frac{3}{7} \div \frac{1}{7} =$

6. $\frac{2}{5} \div \frac{1}{2} =$

7. $\frac{3}{6} \div \frac{1}{2} =$

8. $\frac{2}{8} \div \frac{1}{4} =$

9. $\frac{2}{3} \div \frac{4}{6} =$

10. $\frac{1}{4} \div \frac{4}{1} =$

11. $\frac{2}{7} \div \frac{7}{2} =$

12. $\frac{5}{9} \div \frac{9}{5} =$

13. $\frac{6}{4} \div \frac{1}{3} =$

14. $\frac{5}{8} \div \frac{8}{2} =$

15. $\frac{7}{6} \div \frac{3}{2} =$

16. $\frac{8}{12} \div \frac{1}{2} =$

17. $\frac{8}{12} \div \frac{2}{1} =$

18. $\frac{4}{10} \div \frac{4}{2} =$

19. $\frac{6}{3} \div \frac{3}{1} =$

20. $\frac{14}{20} \div \frac{1}{2} =$

21. $\frac{6}{14} \div \frac{3}{7} =$

22. $\frac{4}{6} \div \frac{2}{4} =$

23. $\frac{3}{4} \div \frac{1}{8} =$

24. $\frac{3}{15} \div \frac{1}{3} =$

25. $\frac{1}{2} \div \frac{1}{3} =$

26. $\frac{1}{4} \div \frac{1}{2} =$

27. $\frac{1}{8} \div \frac{1}{3} =$

28. $\frac{4}{9} \div \frac{4}{8} =$

Practice 15 ☙ ➰ ☙ ☙ ➰ ☙ ➰ ☙ ➰ ☙

> ### Reminder
> - If the numerator is less than half of the denominator, round down.
> - If the numerator is equal to or greater than half of the denominator, round up.
>
> To round $3\frac{3}{8}$ to the nearest whole number, look at the numerator of the fraction part.
> $\frac{3}{8}$ is less than $\frac{1}{2}$ because 3 is less than half of 8. So $3\frac{3}{8}$ rounds down to 3.
> To round $3\frac{4}{5}$ to the nearest whole number, look at the numerator of the fraction part.
> $\frac{4}{5}$ is greater than $\frac{1}{2}$ because 4 is greater than half of 5. So $3\frac{4}{5}$ rounds up to 4.

Directions: Round each fraction or mixed number to the nearest whole number. Use these rounded values to estimate the sums or differences to the nearest whole number. The first two are done for you.

1. $3\frac{1}{3}$ (3)
$+ 1\frac{5}{8}$ $+ (2)$
——— ———
        5

2. $5\frac{1}{5}$ (5)
$- 2\frac{7}{9}$ $- (3)$
——— ———
        2

3. $4\frac{7}{8}$
$+ 3\frac{1}{5}$
———

4. $\frac{4}{7}$
$+ 3\frac{1}{3}$
———

5. $7\frac{1}{6}$
$- 2\frac{3}{4}$
———

6. $4\frac{1}{12}$
$+ \frac{1}{2}$
———

7. $\frac{3}{5}$
$+ 1\frac{1}{2}$
———

8. $4\frac{7}{12}$
$- 2\frac{9}{10}$
———

9. $12\frac{2}{3}$
$- 4\frac{3}{6}$
———

10. $2\frac{1}{10}$
$+ 3\frac{2}{9}$
———

11. $9\frac{8}{10}$
$- 3\frac{1}{5}$
———

12. $3\frac{5}{6}$
$- 1\frac{7}{8}$
———

Directions: Round each fraction or mixed number to the nearest whole number. Use these rounded values to estimate the products or quotients to the nearest whole number. Two problems are done for you.

13. $2\frac{3}{4} \times 7 =$
$(3) \times 7 = 21$

14. $3\frac{4}{5} \times \frac{2}{3} =$

15. $6\frac{1}{2} \times \frac{3}{4} =$

16. $5\frac{1}{5} \times \frac{7}{8} =$

17. $2\frac{8}{9} \times \frac{2}{3} =$

18. $\frac{3}{4} \times 8\frac{1}{3} =$

19. $6\frac{1}{4} \div 3 =$
$(6) \div 3 = 2$

20. $5\frac{9}{10} \div 6 =$

21. $2\frac{9}{10} \div 3 =$

22. $4\frac{5}{6} \div 1 =$

23. $7\frac{7}{10} \div 2 =$

24. $9\frac{1}{5} \div 3 =$

Practice 16 🐚 🌀 🐚 🐚 🌀 🐚 🌀 🐚 🌀 🐚 🌀 🐚

Reminder

Fractions can be converted to decimals by dividing the numerator by the denominator.

Examples:

$$\frac{1}{4} = \begin{array}{r} 0.25 \\ 4\overline{)1.00} \\ -8 \\ \hline 20 \\ -20 \\ \hline 0 \end{array} \qquad \frac{2}{3} = \begin{array}{r} 0.666 \\ 3\overline{)2.000} \\ -18 \\ \hline 20 \\ -18 \\ \hline 20 \end{array} \text{(repeating pattern)} \qquad \frac{3}{5} = \begin{array}{r} 0.6 \\ 5\overline{)3.0} \\ -30 \\ \hline 0 \end{array}$$

Directions: Convert these fractions to decimals. The first two problems are done for you. Use up to three zeroes in the dividend.

1. $\frac{3}{4} =$
$$\begin{array}{r} 0.75 \\ 4\overline{)3.00} \\ -28 \\ \hline 20 \\ -20 \\ \hline 0 \end{array}$$

2. $\frac{1}{8} =$
$$\begin{array}{r} 0.125 \\ 8\overline{)1.000} \\ -8 \\ \hline 20 \\ -16 \\ \hline 40 \\ -40 \\ \hline 0 \end{array}$$

3. $\frac{1}{2} =$
$$2\overline{)1.0}$$

4. $\frac{7}{8} =$

5. $\frac{4}{5} =$

6. $\frac{5}{10} =$

7. $\frac{7}{10} =$

8. $\frac{1}{5} =$

9. $\frac{1}{3} =$

10. $\frac{4}{10} =$

11. $\frac{13}{20} =$

12. $\frac{4}{8} =$

13. $\frac{4}{6} =$

14. $\frac{9}{12} =$

15. $\frac{5}{6} =$

16. $\frac{1}{9} =$

17. $\frac{4}{9} =$

18. $\frac{3}{8} =$

19. $\frac{1}{7} =$

20. $\frac{1}{12} =$

Practice 17

Reminder

Decimals are fractions expressed in tenths, hundredths, thousandths, and other multiples of tenths.

In the number 325.467

  3 = **hundreds** place   4 = **tenths** place
  2 = **tens** place   6 = **hundredths** place
  5 = **ones** place   7 = **thousandths** place

Sample Decimal and Fraction Values

$0.1 = \frac{1}{10} = $ one-tenth

$0.01 = \frac{1}{100} = $ one-hundredth

$0.001 = \frac{1}{1000} = $ one-thousandth

$2.2 = 2\frac{2}{10} = $ two and two-tenths

Directions: Give the fractional value or mixed number for each decimal listed below. The first two are done for you.

1. $0.3 = \underline{\quad \frac{3}{10} \quad}$

2. $1.04 = \underline{\quad 1\frac{4}{100} \quad}$

3. $1.06 = \underline{\qquad}$

4. $0.005 = \underline{\qquad}$

5. $0.9 = \underline{\qquad}$

6. $0.008 = \underline{\qquad}$

7. $1.25 = \underline{\qquad}$

8. $0.007 = \underline{\qquad}$

9. $1.34 = \underline{\qquad}$

10. $3.004 = \underline{\qquad}$

11. $4.06 = \underline{\qquad}$

12. $1.098 = \underline{\qquad}$

13. $3.25 = \underline{\qquad}$

14. $4.007 = \underline{\qquad}$

15. $3.019 = \underline{\qquad}$

16. $1.001 = \underline{\qquad}$

17. $1.1 = \underline{\qquad}$

18. $1.11 = \underline{\qquad}$

19. $1.111 = \underline{\qquad}$

20. $2.02 = \underline{\qquad}$

21. $3.031 = \underline{\qquad}$

22. $23.005 = \underline{\qquad}$

23. $16.004 = \underline{\qquad}$

24. $36.007 = \underline{\qquad}$

25. $11.678 = \underline{\qquad}$

26. $22.234 = \underline{\qquad}$

27. $33.509 = \underline{\qquad}$

28. $0.014 = \underline{\qquad}$

29. $0.777 = \underline{\qquad}$

30. $1.071 = \underline{\qquad}$

31. $4.004 = \underline{\qquad}$

32. $0.405 = \underline{\qquad}$

33. $8.088 = \underline{\qquad}$

Practice 18 ◔ ◔ ◔ ◔ ◔ ◔ ◔ ◔ ◔ ◔ ◔ ◔ ◔

> ### Reminder
> Decimals are fractions expressed in tenths, hundredths, thousandths, and other multiples of tenths.
>
> **In the number 325.467**
> 3 = hundreds   4 = tenths
> 2 = tens   6 = hundredths
> 5 = ones   7 = thousandths
> (three hundred twenty-five and
> four hundred sixty-seven thousandths)
>
> **Reading Decimal Values**
> 0.3 = three-tenths
> 0.34 = thirty-four hundredths
> 0.013 = thirteen-thousandths
> 5.123 = five and one hundred twenty-three thousandths
> The word "and" represents the decimal.

Directions: Write in words the value of each decimal listed below. The first two are done for you.

1. 0.045 _____ forty-five thousandths _____
2. 23.12 _twenty-three and twelve hundredths_
3. 0.415 _____
4. 0.03 _____
5. 0.34 _____
6. 0.16 _____
7. 3.005 _____
8. 1.09 _____
9. 2.007 _____
10. 2.08 _____
11. 41.14 _____
12. 7.081 _____
13. 4.001 _____
14. 2.101 _____
15. 5.132 _____
16. 3.026 _____
17. 5.110 _____
18. 19.006 _____
19. 1.020 _____
20. 9.99 _____
21. 9.999 _____
22. 9.909 _____
23. 4.203 _____
24. 6.666 _____

Practice 19

> ## Reminder
>
> - The location of a digit in a decimal determines its value.
>
>   In the number **325.467**
>
> | | |
> |---|---|
> | **3** = **hundreds** place | **4** = **tenths** place |
> | **2** = **tens** place | **6** = **hundredths** place |
> | **5** = **ones** place | **7** = **thousandths** place |
>
> - Each place to the left in the number line is valued at 10 times as much as the place to its right.
> - Each place to the right in the number line is valued at one-tenth as much as the place to its left.

Directions: Compare the value of each decimal pair using > (greater than) or < (less than). The first two are done for you.

1. 0.23 __>__ 0.023   **2.** 1.003 __<__ 1.03   **3.** 2.02 _____ 2.20

4. 1.340 _____ 1.034   **5.** 0.013 _____ 0.031   **6.** 0.016 _____ 0.160

7. 0.003 _____ 0.03   **8.** 4.012 _____ 4.102   **9.** 0.045 _____ 0.540

10. 0.3 _____ 3.0   **11.** 0.04 _____ 0.4   **12.** 3.678 _____ 36.78

13. 2.11 _____ 21.1   **14.** 0.25 _____ 0.025   **15.** 1.6 _____ 0.16

16. 3.11 _____ 0.311   **17.** 35.5 _____ 0.355   **18.** 3.12 _____ 3.21

19. 6.07 _____ 6.7   **20.** 0.067 _____ 0.67   **21.** 6.8 _____ 8.6

22. 6.66 _____ 66.6   **23.** 0.055 _____ 0.5   **24.** 0.44 _____ 4.04

25. 0.123 _____ 0.12   **26.** 0.660 _____ 0.066   **27.** 30.09 _____ 300.9

28. 14.4 _____ 0.144   **29.** 3.41 _____ 0.352   **30.** 1.111 _____ 11.01

31. 0.121 _____ 2   **32.** 4 _____ 3.999   **33.** 6 _____ 5.099

#8630 Practice Makes Perfect: Fractions, Decimals & Percents   ©*Teacher Created Resources, Inc.*

Practice 20

Directions: Place these decimals in order from **least to greatest**. Four sets are done for you.

1. 0.06 _0.06_
0.30 _0.25_
0.25 _0.30_

2. 0.65 _0.50_
0.50 _0.65_
0.90 _0.90_

3. 0.35 _____
0.10 _____
0.2 _____

4. 1.95 _____
0.9 _____
0.09 _____

5. 0.06 _____
0.60 _____
1.05 _____

6. 1.04 _____
2.4 _____
0.24 _____

7. 2 _____
1.61 _____
1.6 _____

8. 1.05 _____
1.50 _____
2.5 _____

9. 0.8 _____
0.79 _____
0.7 _____

10. 1.2 _____
1.02 _____
2.01 _____

11. 1.03 _____
1.5 _____
1.43 _____

12. 2.0 _____
2.01 _____
2.1 _____

13. 3.4 _3.04_
3.04 _3.111_
3.111 _3.4_

14. 5.033 _4.44_
5.5 _5.033_
4.44 _5.5_

15. 1.013 _____
0.11 _____
1.101 _____

16. 6.66 _____
6.6 _____
6.031 _____

17. 7.1 _____
7.17 _____
6.999 _____

18. 5.051 _____
5.15 _____
4.9 _____

19. 1.810 _____
1.18 _____
1.8 _____

20. 3.313 _____
3.101 _____
1.34 _____

21. 3.101 _____
3.011 _____
3.11 _____

22. 1.411 _____
0.412 _____
1.041 _____

23. 5.505 _____
5.55 _____
5.5 _____

24. 3.214 _____
1.244 _____
3.3 _____

25. 1.134 _____
3.41 _____
3.3 _____

26. 6.701 _____
5.999 _____
7.1 _____

27. 0.003 _____
3.303 _____
3.31 _____

28. 3.001 _____
2.9 _____
3.101 _____

29. 5.946 _____
5.95 _____
5.947 _____

30. 6.001 _____
5.9 _____
6.17 _____

Practice 21 ☙ ☙ ☙ ☙ ☙ ☙ ☙ ☙ ☙ ☙ ☙

> ### Reminder
> - To add decimals, arrange the numbers in the ladder form and line up the decimal points.
> - Use placeholder zeroes (if needed).
> - Add the numbers (carry where necessary).
> - Line up the decimal in your answer with the decimals from the problem.
>   Example: $3.241 + 22.9 =$
>
> $$3.241$$
> $$+ 22.900 \leftarrow \text{(placeholder zeroes)}$$
> $$26.141 \leftarrow \text{(decimal stays three places to the left)}$$

Directions: Use the reminder above to correctly add these decimals. The first two are done for you. Use a separate sheet of paper to complete #13–27.

1. $\begin{array}{r} 4.121 \\ + 6.900 \\ \hline 11.021 \end{array}$
2. $\begin{array}{r} 2.883 \\ + 3.300 \\ \hline 6.183 \end{array}$
3. $\begin{array}{r} 0.531 \\ + 0.7 \\ \hline \end{array}$

4. $\begin{array}{r} 9.618 \\ + 9.403 \\ \hline \end{array}$
5. $\begin{array}{r} 0.102 \\ + 0.91 \\ \hline \end{array}$
6. $\begin{array}{r} 9.101 \\ + 17.3 \\ \hline \end{array}$

7. $\begin{array}{r} 0.01 \\ + 7.004 \\ \hline \end{array}$
8. $\begin{array}{r} 9.999 \\ + 0.7 \\ \hline \end{array}$
9. $\begin{array}{r} 5.508 \\ + 95.1 \\ \hline \end{array}$

10. $\begin{array}{r} 8.79 \\ + 0.3 \\ \hline \end{array}$
11. $\begin{array}{r} 0.006 \\ + 6.6 \\ \hline \end{array}$
12. $\begin{array}{r} 9.001 \\ + 9.999 \\ \hline \end{array}$

13. $3.1 + 9.006 =$
14. $1.9 + 0.003 =$
15. $16.78 + 0.008 =$

16. $0.015 + 0.7 =$
17. $1.08 + 0.999 =$
18. $6.1 + 0.008 =$

19. $9.007 + 6.09 =$
20. $40.1 + 0.001 =$
21. $2.01 + 0.1 =$

22. $2.012 + 0.8 =$
23. $1.7 + 0.111 =$
24. $7.6 + 0.006 =$

25. $4.01 + 3 =$
26. $8.2 + 10 =$
27. $50 + 0.2 =$

Practice 22 ✇ ✇ ✇ ✇ ✇ ✇ ✇ ✇ ✇ ✇ ✇

Reminder

To subtract decimals:

1. Use the ladder form.
2. Line up the decimals.
3. Use placeholder zeroes (if needed).
4. Subtract the numbers (borrow/regroup where necessary).
5. Line up the decimal in your answer with the decimals from the problem.

$$8.1 - 6.513 =$$

$$8.\overset{7\ 10\ 9\ 10}{100} \leftarrow \text{(placeholder zeroes)}$$
$$- 6.513$$
$$1.587 \leftarrow \text{(decimal stays three places to the left)}$$

Directions: Use the reminder above to correctly subtract these decimals. The first two are done for you. Use a separate sheet of paper to complete #13–27.

1.
$$\begin{array}{r} 6.100 \\ - 1.834 \\ \hline 4.266 \end{array}$$

2.
$$\begin{array}{r} 0.900 \\ - 0.813 \\ \hline 0.087 \end{array}$$

3.
$$\begin{array}{r} 8.1 \\ - 3.66 \\ \hline \end{array}$$

4.
$$\begin{array}{r} 17.03 \\ - 5.762 \\ \hline \end{array}$$

5.
$$\begin{array}{r} 8.013 \\ - 1.3 \\ \hline \end{array}$$

6.
$$\begin{array}{r} 9.4 \\ - 4.002 \\ \hline \end{array}$$

7.
$$\begin{array}{r} 0.1 \\ - 0.011 \\ \hline \end{array}$$

8.
$$\begin{array}{r} 9 \\ - 5.713 \\ \hline \end{array}$$

9.
$$\begin{array}{r} 4.113 \\ - 2.332 \\ \hline \end{array}$$

10.
$$\begin{array}{r} 3.022 \\ - 1.123 \\ \hline \end{array}$$

11.
$$\begin{array}{r} 5.019 \\ - 1.238 \\ \hline \end{array}$$

12.
$$\begin{array}{r} 8 \\ - 7.188 \\ \hline \end{array}$$

13. $2.1 - 1.08 =$

14. $6 - 4.77 =$

15. $3.01 - 2.897 =$

16. $2 - 0.003 =$

17. $9 - 2.008 =$

18. $42 - 13.078 =$

19. $2.011 - 0.14 =$

20. $20 - 13.002 =$

21. $6.01 - 3.041 =$

22. $7 - 2.421 =$

23. $34.2 - 5.022 =$

24. $13 - 11.91 =$

25. $2 - 0.68 =$

26. $4.1 - 1.071 =$

27. $14 - 1.013 =$

Practice 23

Reminder

When multiplying decimals by multiples of 10, move the decimal to the right as many places as there are zeros.

    Examples: 2.3 x 10 = 23   2.45 x 100 = 245   7.432 x 1,000 = 7,432
Add zeros if needed:
    Examples: 2.3 x 100 = 230   2.3 x 1,000 = 2,300

Directions: Multiply the decimals in these problems. The first three are done for you.

1. 3.4 x 10 = _____34_____   **2.** 2.8 x 100 = _____280_____   **3.** 4.5 x 1,000 = ___4,500___

4. 5.7 x 10 = _____   **5.** 9.6 x 10 = _____   **6.** 1.4 x 100 = _____

7. 5.1 x 10 = _____   **8.** 0.23 x 100 = _____   **9.** 0.1 x 10 = _____

10. 0.2 x 100 = _____   **11.** 0.09 x 100 = _____   **12.** 0.005 x 1,000 = _____

13. 0.6 x 100 = _____   **14.** 0.112 x 10 = _____   **15.** 1.12 x 1,000 = _____

16. 11.22 x 100 = _____   **17.** 21.3 x 10 = _____   **18.** 32.3 x 1,000 = _____

19. 0.001 x 10 = _____   **20.** 0.001 x 100 = _____   **21.** 0.001 x 1,000 = _____

22. 0.2 x 1,000 = _____   **23.** 7.77 x 10 = _____   **24.** 66.6 x 100 = _____

25. 100 x 55.55 = _____   **26.** 10 x 0.88 = _____   **27.** 100 x 3.414 = _____

28. 10 x 3.01 = _____   **29.** 100 x 0.2 = _____   **30.** 1,000 x 0.03 = _____

31. 100 x 0.14 = _____   **32.** 10 x 2.45 = _____   **33.** 1,000 x 0.15 = _____

34. 1,000 x 1.1 = _____   **35.** 100 x 28.1 = _____   **36.** 10 x 299.5 = _____

Practice 24 🌀 ∂ ∂ 🌀 🌀 ∂ 🌀 ∂ 🌀 ∂ 🌀

Reminder

When you multiply decimals by decimals:
1. Do the standard multiplication process.
2. Count the total number of places to the right of the decimals in the problem.
3. Leave the same number of places to the right of the decimal in the product (answer).
    Examples: $0.03 \times 0.5 = 0.015$ $0.0004 \times 0.9 = 0.00036$

Directions: Multiply these decimals. Determine where the decimal goes in the answer. The first two are done for you. Use another sheet of paper to show your work.

1.   2.1
   x 1.1
   ───
    21
   +210
   ───
   2.31

2.   0.79
   x 0.011
   ───
     79
   + 790
   ───
   0.00869

3.   1.84
   x 0.03

4.   3.2
   x   4.4

5.   0.981
   x 0.004

6.   1.35
   x .22

7.   0.67
   x 0.33

8.   1.239
   x 4.340

9.   0.7891
   x   0.276

10.   7.796
   x   1.12

11.   0.123
   x   2.5

12.   78.9
   x   44

13.   345
   x 0.10

14.   2.1111
   x   9

15.   5678
   x 0.01

16.   98.5
   x   .4

17.   0.0006
   x   3.1

18.   30,010
   x   2.2

19.   0.765
   x   0.9

20.   567.8
   x   4.56

21.   8,010.5
   x   4.44

22.   0.0009
   x   0.8

23.   2.223
   x 3.03

24.   1,929.1
   x   1.2

Practice 25 🐚 ᥲ 🐚 🐚 ᥲ 🐚 ᥲ 🐚 ᥲ 🐚

Reminder

When dividing decimals by multiples of 10, move the decimal to the left as many places as there are zeroes.

Examples: $1.3 \div 10 = 0.13$ $166 \div 100 = 1.66$ $849.1 \div 1{,}000 = 0.8491$

Add zeroes if needed:

Examples: $3.3 \div 100 = 0.033$ $9.8 \div 1{,}000 = 0.0098$

Directions: Divide the decimals in these problems. The first three are done for you.

1. $5.4 \div 10 = \underline{\quad 0.54 \quad}$ 2. $3.78 \div 100 = \underline{\quad 0.0378 \quad}$ 3. $0.9 \div 1{,}000 = \underline{\quad 0.0009 \quad}$

4. $6.78 \div 10 = \underline{\qquad\qquad}$ 5. $8.9 \div 1{,}000 = \underline{\qquad\qquad}$ 6. $0.078 \div 100 = \underline{\qquad\qquad}$

7. $67.01 \div 100 = \underline{\qquad\qquad}$ 8. $5.4 \div 100 = \underline{\qquad\qquad}$ 9. $16.1 \div 100 = \underline{\qquad\qquad}$

10. $889.1 \div 10 = \underline{\qquad\qquad}$ 11. $4.1 \div 100 = \underline{\qquad\qquad}$ 12. $45 \div 1{,}000 = \underline{\qquad\qquad}$

Directions: Divide these numerals by 10, 100, and 1,000. The first three are done for you.

13. $\dfrac{44}{100} = \underline{\quad 0.44 \quad}$ 14. $\dfrac{886}{1{,}000} = \underline{\quad 0.886 \quad}$ 15. $\dfrac{354}{10} = \underline{\quad 35.4 \quad}$

16. $\dfrac{56}{100} = \underline{\qquad\qquad}$ 17. $\dfrac{5}{10} = \underline{\qquad\qquad}$ 18. $\dfrac{456}{1{,}000} = \underline{\qquad\qquad}$

19. $\dfrac{778}{1{,}000} = \underline{\qquad\qquad}$ 20. $\dfrac{3}{1{,}000} = \underline{\qquad\qquad}$ 21. $\dfrac{2{,}345}{10} = \underline{\qquad\qquad}$

22. $\dfrac{20}{100} = \underline{\qquad\qquad}$ 23. $\dfrac{5}{100} = \underline{\qquad\qquad}$ 24. $\dfrac{3{,}145}{1{,}000} = \underline{\qquad\qquad}$

25. $\dfrac{10}{100} = \underline{\qquad\qquad}$ 26. $\dfrac{10}{1{,}000} = \underline{\qquad\qquad}$ 27. $\dfrac{1}{10} = \underline{\qquad\qquad}$

Practice 26

Reminder

When dividing a decimal by a whole number:
1. Do the standard division process.
2. Add zeroes to the dividend, if necessary, to avoid having a remainder.
3. Place the decimal in the quotient (answer), directly above the decimal in the dividend.

$$4)\overline{32.8} \quad = 8.2$$
$$-32$$
$$\quad 8$$
$$-\;8$$
$$\quad 0$$

$$5)\overline{47.2} \quad = 9.4\,r2$$
$$-45$$
$$\quad22$$
$$-20$$
$$\quad2$$

$$5)\overline{47.20} \quad = 9.44$$
$$-45$$
$$\quad22$$
$$-20$$
$$\quad20$$
$$-20$$
$$\quad0$$

Directions: Divide these decimals by whole numbers. Use the examples above to help you.

1. $6)\overline{6.36}$

2. $25)\overline{105.5}$

3. $7)\overline{49.14}$

4. $12)\overline{1.44}$

5. $9)\overline{63.36}$

6. $11)\overline{12.1}$

7. $13)\overline{1.69}$

8. $6)\overline{7.236}$

9. $15)\overline{22.5}$

10. $4)\overline{34.2}$

11. $8)\overline{6.8}$

12. $25)\overline{7.55}$

13. $12)\overline{12.6}$

14. $15)\overline{9.6}$

15. $18)\overline{5.49}$

16. $9)\overline{3.681}$

17. $22)\overline{1.10}$

18. $25)\overline{40.5}$

19. $16)\overline{4.832}$

20. $35)\overline{10.57}$

21. $12)\overline{7.26}$

Practice 27 🐚 🐚 🐚 🐚 🐚 🐚 🐚 🐚 🐚 🐚 🐚

Reminder

When dividing decimals by decimals:

1. Move the decimal in the divisor (outside the division sign) to the right, making it a whole number.
2. Move the decimal in the dividend (inside the division sign) the same number of places to the right.
3. Add zeroes to the dividend, if necessary.
4. Put the decimal in the quotient (answer) directly above the decimal in the dividend.
5. Do the standard division process.

Examples:

$$.05\overline{)4.55} = 05.\overline{)455.}^{\;91.} \qquad .35\overline{)70.7} = 35.\overline{)7070.}^{\;202.}$$

Directions: Solve these division problems. Follow the steps listed above. Add additional zeroes in the dividend, if needed.

1. $.3\overline{)24.3}$

2. $.15\overline{)30.15}$

3. $.4\overline{)1.62}$

4. $.24\overline{)4.8}$

5. $.6\overline{)1.224}$

6. $.006\overline{)0.126}$

7. $.008\overline{)2.4}$

8. $.15\overline{)45.6}$

9. $.55\overline{)11.055}$

10. $.9\overline{)1.881}$

11. $.16\overline{)3.2}$

12. $.0004\overline{)8.4}$

13. $.002\overline{)4.8}$

14. $.0007\overline{)7.7}$

15. $.00003\overline{)6}$

16. $0.013\overline{)3.9}$

17. $0.025\overline{)7.5}$

18. $0.20\overline{)4.4}$

Practice 28 ☙ ᕫ ᕫ ☙ ☙ ᕫ ☙ ᕫ ☙ ᕫ ☙

Reminder

- Terminating decimals have a limited number of digits and no remainder in the quotient.
- Repeating decimals repeat one or more digits in the same pattern infinitely (forever).
- Irrational numbers cannot be expressed as a fraction and do not have a repeating pattern of digits in the quotient.

Terminating Decimal:	$\dfrac{5.02}{5)\,25.10}$	(no remainder)
Repeating Decimal:	.666... $3)\,2.000$ $-\,18$ $\quad 20$	(repeating pattern) (non-terminating)
Irrational Number:	3.1428571...	(no number pattern) (non-terminating)

Directions: Complete these division problems. Label each quotient as terminating or repeating. The first two are done for you.

1.
```
       .66
  6) 4.00
   - 36
      40
    - 36
      40
```
repeating

2.
```
       2.10
  4) 8.40
   - 8
      4
    - 4
      0
```
terminating

3.
```
  3) 1.000
```

4.
```
  8) 5.000
```

5.
```
  9) 4.000
```

6.
```
  8) 6.000
```

7.
```
  9) 7.000
```

8.
```
  9) 8.000
```

9.
```
  6) 5.0000
```

Directions: Label these decimals as terminating (T), repeating (R), or irrational (I).

10. 3.45 _____

11. 1.125 _____

12. 0.3333... _____

13. 0.428571428... _____

14. 0.173648... _____

15. 0.181818... _____

16. 1.73205008... _____

17. 0.9333... _____

Practice 29

Reminder

- Percent means "of 100."
- All percents are fractional parts of 100.
- This sign means percent: %
- The shaded part of the graph shows 38% because 38 of the 100 squares are shaded. This means that 62% is not shaded.

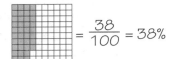

Directions: Write the percent shaded next to each graph.

1.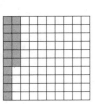

2.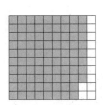

3.

4.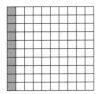

5.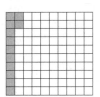

6.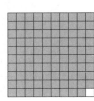

7.

8.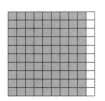

9.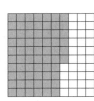

10.

11.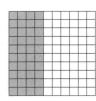

12.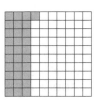

13.

14.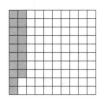

15.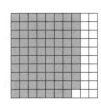

16.

17.

18.

Practice 30 🌀 🌀 🌀 🌀 🌀 🌀 🌀 🌀 🌀 🌀 🌀

Reminder

Decimals in the hundredths places are converted to percents by removing the decimal point and adding the percent sign. Drop unnecessary zeroes.

$$0.25 = 25\% \qquad 0.03 = 3\% \qquad 0.12 = 12\%$$

Decimals in the thousandths places are converted to percents by moving the decimal point two places to the right and adding the percent sign. Drop unnecessary zeroes.

$$0.025 = 2.5\% \qquad 0.003 = .3\% \qquad 0.095 = 9.5\%$$

NOTE: Some zero placeholders must be added, as in these examples:

$$6.9 = 690\% \qquad 10.4 = 1040\% \qquad 9.5 = 950\%$$

Directions: Convert the following decimals into percents. The first two are done for you.

1. 0.35 = _____35%_____

2. 4.02 = _____402%_____

3. 0.04 = _____

4. 0.02 = _____

5. 0.91 = _____

6. 1.07 = _____

7. 1.09 = _____

8. 0.08 = _____

9. 17.06 = _____

10. 0.13 = _____

11. 0.01 = _____

12. 2.39 = _____

13. 0.005 = _____

14. 0.012 = _____

15. 9.003 = _____

16. 1.01 = _____

17. 3.001 = _____

18. 7.7 = _____

Directions: Convert these percents to decimals. The first two are done for you.

19. 24% = _____0.24_____

20. 2.3% = _____0.023_____

21. 9.08% = _____

22. 3.4% = _____

23. 90.13% = _____

24. 6.4% = _____

25. 44% = _____

26. 19.4% = _____

27. 1.1% = _____

28. 1.13% = _____

29. 4% = _____

30. 82.5% = _____

31. 7% = _____

32. 1.03% = _____

33. 1% = _____

Practice 31 ꩜ ꩜ ꩜ ꩜ ꩜ ꩜ ꩜ ꩜ ꩜ ꩜ ꩜

Reminder

Fractions are converted to percents by dividing the numerator by the denominator, adding two or more zeroes, and writing the percent sign.

Examples:

$$\frac{1}{4} = 4\overline{)1.00} \quad \frac{.25 = 25\%}{}$$
$$\begin{array}{r} -\ 8 \\ \hline 20 \\ -20 \\ \hline 0 \end{array}$$

$$\frac{1}{3} = 3\overline{)1.000} \quad \frac{.333 = 33.3\%}{}$$
$$\begin{array}{r} -\ 9 \\ \hline 10 \\ -\ 9 \\ \hline 10 \end{array}$$

Directions: Convert these fractions to percents. The first two are done for you.

1. $\frac{1}{2} = 2\overline{)1.00} \quad .50 = 50\%$
$$\begin{array}{r} -\ 10 \\ \hline 0 \end{array}$$

1. $\frac{2}{7} = 7\overline{)2.000} \quad .285 = 28.5\%$
$$\begin{array}{r} -\ 14 \\ \hline 60 \\ -\ 56 \\ \hline 40 \\ -\ 35 \\ \hline 5 \end{array}$$

3. $\frac{4}{8} = 8\overline{)4.00}$

4. $\frac{3}{4} =$

5. $\frac{5}{8} =$

6. $\frac{4}{10} =$

7. $\frac{7}{9} =$

8. $\frac{12}{20} =$

9. $\frac{1}{4} =$

10. $\frac{3}{11} =$

11. $\frac{4}{18} =$

12. $\frac{5}{10} =$

13. $\frac{6}{30} =$

14. $\frac{1}{10} =$

15. $\frac{4}{5} =$

Practice 32

Reminder

Percents are converted to fractions in terms of tenths, hundredths, or thousandths and reduced to lowest terms.

$$28\% = \frac{28}{100} = \frac{7}{25} \qquad 19\% = \frac{19}{100} \qquad 30\% = \frac{30}{100} = \frac{3}{10} \qquad 66.7\% = \frac{667}{1,000}$$

Directions: Convert these percents to fractions and reduce. The first three are done for you. (Some fractions cannot be reduced.)

1. $40\% = \frac{40}{100} = \frac{2}{5}$

2. $25\% = \frac{25}{100} = \frac{1}{4}$

3. $33.3\% = \frac{333}{1,000}$

4. $16\% = $ _____

5. $99\% = $ _____

6. $43.3\% = $ _____

7. $18\% = $ _____

8. $77\% = $ _____

9. $20\% = $ _____

10. $29\% = $ _____

11. $14\% = $ _____

12. $16.9\% = $ _____

13. $6\% = $ _____

14. $35\% = $ _____

15. $13.5\% = $ _____

16. $9\% = $ _____

17. $14.9\% = $ _____

18. $3.2\% = \frac{32}{1,000} = $ _____

19. $44\% = $ _____

20. $99.9\% = $ _____

21. $1\% = $ _____

22. $90\% = $ _____

23. $65\% = $ _____

24. $12.9\% = $ _____

25. $11\% = $ _____

26. $36\% = $ _____

27. $19.9\% = $ _____

28. $11.1\% = $ _____

29. $55\% = $ _____

30. $70.7\% = $ _____

Practice 33

Reminder

Compute percents by changing the percent to an equivalent decimal and then multiply.

$$33\% \text{ of } 15 = \begin{array}{r} 15 \\ \times\ .33 \\ \hline 45 \\ +450 \\ \hline 4.95 \end{array} = 4.95 \qquad 12\% \text{ of } 40 = \begin{array}{r} 40 \\ \times\ .12 \\ \hline 80 \\ +400 \\ \hline 4.80 \end{array} = 4.8$$

Convert percents to fractions and then multiply.

$$50\% \text{ of } 18 = \frac{1}{2} \times 18 = 9 \qquad 25\% \text{ of } 40 = \frac{1}{4} \times 40 = 10$$

Directions: Compute these percents by converting the percent to a decimal and then multiplying. The first two are done for you.

1. 9% of 50 =
$$\begin{array}{r} 50 \\ \times\ .09 \\ \hline 4.50 \end{array} = 4.5$$

2. 12% of 60 =
$$\begin{array}{r} 60 \\ \times\ .12 \\ \hline 120 \\ +600 \\ \hline 7.20 \end{array} = 7.2$$

3. 20% of 18 =
$$\begin{array}{r} 18 \\ \times\ .20 \\ \hline \end{array}$$

4. 66% of 100 =

5. 8% of 200 =

6. 13% of 40 =

7. 8% of 80 =

8. 16% of 40 =

9. 22% of 70 =

10. 94% of 300 =

11. 5% of 500 =

12. 2% of 140 =

Directions: Convert these percents to fractions and then multiply. The first one is done for you.

13. 50% of 80 =
$$\frac{1}{2} \times 80 = 40$$

14. 25% of 200 =

15. 10% of 60 =

16. 90% of 60 =

17. 20% of 400 =

18. 75% of 40 =

19. 50% of 160 =

20. 30% of 800 =

Practice 34 🐚 🌀 🐚 🐚 🌀 🐚 🌀 🐚 🌀 🐚

Directions: Compute the discount for each problem and the actual cost. The first two are done for you. Use a separate sheet of paper for your calculations, if needed.

1. $30 haircut; 20% discount

   Discount = ___$30 x .20 = $6___

   Actual cost = ___$30 – $6 = $24___

2. $90 CD player; 30% discount

   Discount = ___$90 x .30 = $27___

   Actual cost = ___$90 – $27 = $63___

3. $50 concert ticket; 25% discount

   Discount = _____

   Actual cost: _____

4. $25 dinner at restaurant; 10% discount

   Discount = _____

   Actual cost = _____

5. $46 tennis shoes; 15% discount

   Discount = _____

   Actual cost: _____

6. $100 airline ticket; 35% discount

   Discount = _____

   Actual cost = _____

7. $66 coat; 22% discount

   Discount = _____

   Actual cost: _____

8. $78 video game; 9% discount

   Discount = _____

   Actual cost = _____

9. $28 DVD; 8% discount

   Discount = _____

   Actual cost: _____

10. $320 TV; 30% discount

    Discount = _____

    Actual cost = _____

11. $15 book; 6% discount

    Discount = _____

    Actual cost: _____

12. $62 sweater; 15% discount

    Discount = _____

    Actual cost = _____

13. $12 lunch; 5% discount

    Discount = _____

    Actual cost: _____

14. $88 bike; 25% discount

    Discount = _____

    Actual cost = _____

15. $14 pizza; 10% discount

    Discount = _____

    Actual cost: _____

16. $62 ring; 20% discount

    Discount = _____

    Actual cost = _____

Practice 35 ✆ ❧ ❧ ✆ ✆ ❧ ✆ ❧ ✆ ❧ ✆

Reminder

Compute sales prices by converting the percentage to a decimal and multiplying. Then subtract the amount from the original price.

Example: (Store #1) Original price $41.95 plus a 20%-off sale
$41.95 x 0.20 = $8.39 (amount of discount)
Actual cost: $41.95 – $8.39 = $33.56

Best deal: Store #1 has the best deal on this item.

(Store #2) Original price $77.49 plus a 30%-off sale
$77.49 x 0.30 = $23.25 (amount of discount)
Actual cost: $77.49 – $23.25 = $54.24

Directions: Compute the discount for each item and the actual cost from both stores. Decide which store has the best deal. The first one is done for you. Use a separate sheet of paper for your calculations, if needed.

1. (Store #1) $48 jeans at 30% off
   _____$48 x 0.30 = $14.40_____ discount
   Actual Cost: ___$48 – $14.40 = $33.60___
   Best deal: _Store #1 has the best deal on these jeans._

   (Store #2) $75 jeans at 40% off
   ___$75 x 0.40 = $30___ discount
   Actual Cost: ___$75 – $30 = $45___

2. (Store #1) $80 skateboard at 22% off
   _____ discount
   Actual Cost: _____
   Best deal: _____

   (Store #2) $95 skateboard at 25% off
   _____ discount
   Actual Cost: _____

3. (Store #1) $100 coat at 23% off
   _____ discount
   Actual Cost: _____
   Best deal: _____

   (Store #2) $71 coat at 12% off
   _____ discount
   Actual Cost: _____

4. (Store #1) $213 bike at 30% off
   _____ discount
   Actual Cost: _____
   Best deal: _____

   (Store #2) $190 bike at 20% off
   _____ discount
   Actual Cost: _____

5. (Store #1) $9 basketball at 40% off
   _____ discount
   Actual Cost: _____
   Best deal: _____

   (Store #2) $15 basketball at 60% off
   _____ discount
   Actual Cost: _____

6. (Store #1) $1.75 candy at 40% off
   _____ discount
   Actual Cost: _____
   Best deal: _____

   (Store #2) $2.40 candy at 60% off
   _____ discount
   Actual Cost: _____

7. (Store #1) $8 shirt at 15% off
   _____ discount
   Actual Cost: _____
   Best deal: _____

   (Store #2) $11 shirt at 25% off
   _____ discount
   Actual Cost: _____

Practice 36 ✆ ➲ ✆ ✆ ➲ ✆ ➲ ✆ ➲ ✆

> ### Reminder
> - The formula for computing simple interest is I = P x R x T (Interest = Principal x Rate x Time).
> - **Principal** is the amount of money on loan.
> - **Rate** is the percentage you earn or pay.
> - **Time** is the amount of time you borrow or save the principal in years.
>   Example: You borrow $1,000 at a 20%-rate for 2 years
>   (I = P x R x T) I = $1,000 x 0.20 x 2 = $400
>   You will pay back $1,000 plus $400 in interest = a total of $1,400

Directions: Compute the interest and total payment for each problem below. The first one is done for you.

1. Loan of $2,000

   25% rate for 2 years

   Interest = ___$2,000 x 0.25 x 2 = $1,000___

   Total payment = $2,000 + $1,000 = $3,000

2. Loan of $500

   22% rate for 1 year

   Interest = $500 x 0.22 x 1 = _____

   Total payment = _____

3. Loan of $4,000

   20% rate for 1 year

   Interest = _____

   Total payment = _____

4. Deposit of $2,500

   10% rate for 1 year

   Interest = _____

   Total deposit = _____

5. Loan of $10,000

   21% rate for 5 years

   Interest = _____

   Total payment = _____

6. Loan of $3,000

   15% rate for 3 years

   Interest = _____

   Total deposit = _____

7. Deposit of $5,000

   8% rate for 3 years

   Interest = _____

   Total deposit = _____

8. Deposit of $1,200

   11% rate for 2 years

   Interest = _____

   Total deposit = _____

9. Loan of $40,000

   8% rate for 20 years

   Interest = _____

   Total payment = _____

10. Loan of $55,000

    9% rate for 10 years

    Interest = _____

    Total deposit = _____

Test Practice 1

Directions: Identify the equivalent fraction for each fraction listed.

1. $\frac{2}{3} =$
      (A) $\frac{4}{8}$ (B) $\frac{3}{6}$ (C) $\frac{7}{9}$ (D) $\frac{8}{12}$

2. $\frac{10}{12} =$
      (A) $\frac{2}{3}$ (B) $\frac{3}{4}$ (C) $\frac{5}{6}$ (D) $\frac{5}{8}$

3. $\frac{4}{7} =$
      (A) $\frac{8}{14}$ (B) $\frac{3}{5}$ (C) $\frac{10}{12}$ (D) $\frac{8}{11}$

4. $\frac{1}{4}$
      (A) $\frac{3}{8}$ (B) $\frac{2}{6}$ (C) $\frac{2}{8}$ (D) $\frac{4}{10}$

5. $\frac{3}{8} =$
      (A) $\frac{1}{4}$ (B) $\frac{6}{16}$ (C) $\frac{6}{14}$ (D) $\frac{1}{2}$

6. $\frac{6}{9} =$
      (A) $\frac{2}{3}$ (B) $\frac{1}{2}$ (C) $\frac{12}{16}$ (D) $\frac{5}{8}$

Directions: Change these improper fractions to mixed numbers.

7. $\frac{9}{5} =$
      (A) $1\frac{3}{5}$ (B) $1\frac{1}{4}$ (C) $1\frac{4}{9}$ (D) $1\frac{4}{5}$

8. $\frac{11}{8} =$
      (A) $1\frac{1}{4}$ (B) $1\frac{3}{8}$ (C) $1\frac{1}{8}$ (D) $1\frac{1}{3}$

9. $\frac{9}{2} =$
      (A) $3\frac{1}{2}$ (B) $2\frac{1}{2}$ (C) $4\frac{1}{9}$ (D) $4\frac{1}{2}$

10. $\frac{12}{7} =$
      (A) $1\frac{1}{7}$ (B) $1\frac{7}{12}$ (C) $1\frac{5}{12}$ (D) $1\frac{5}{7}$

11. $\frac{13}{3} =$
      (A) $4\frac{1}{2}$ (B) $3\frac{2}{3}$ (C) $4\frac{1}{3}$ (D) $4\frac{1}{13}$

12. $\frac{7}{3} =$
      (A) $1\frac{2}{7}$ (B) $2\frac{3}{7}$ (C) $1\frac{4}{7}$ (D) $2\frac{1}{3}$

Directions: Reduce these fractions to lowest terms.

13. $\frac{10}{15} =$
      (A) $\frac{1}{3}$ (B) $\frac{2}{5}$ (C) $\frac{2}{3}$ (D) $\frac{3}{5}$

14. $\frac{9}{21} =$
      (A) $\frac{3}{12}$ (B) $\frac{3}{7}$ (C) $\frac{4}{10}$ (D) $\frac{3}{8}$

15. $\frac{10}{18} =$
      (A) $\frac{2}{3}$ (B) $\frac{5}{9}$ (C) $\frac{5}{8}$ (D) $\frac{2}{8}$

16. $\frac{11}{33} =$
      (A) $\frac{1}{3}$ (B) $\frac{2}{11}$ (C) $\frac{2}{3}$ (D) $\frac{1}{5}$

17. $\frac{12}{27} =$
      (A) $\frac{1}{3}$ (B) $\frac{4}{9}$ (C) $\frac{3}{9}$ (D) $\frac{9}{12}$

18. $\frac{16}{28} =$
      (A) $\frac{1}{2}$ (B) $\frac{2}{7}$ (C) $\frac{4}{7}$ (D) $\frac{4}{9}$

19. $\frac{13}{39} =$
      (A) $\frac{1}{13}$ (B) $\frac{1}{3}$ (C) $\frac{6}{20}$ (D) $\frac{4}{11}$

20. $\frac{14}{22} =$
      (A) $\frac{1}{2}$ (B) $\frac{8}{11}$ (C) $\frac{7}{13}$ (D) $\frac{7}{11}$

Test Practice 2

Directions: Determine the lowest common denominator (LCD) for each pair of fractions.

1. $\frac{2}{3}$ and $\frac{3}{4}$

    Ⓐ 9   Ⓑ 4   Ⓒ 12   Ⓓ 15

2. $\frac{1}{2}$ and $\frac{3}{6}$

    Ⓐ 3   Ⓑ 12   Ⓒ 18   Ⓓ 6

3. $\frac{2}{5}$ and $\frac{3}{4}$

    Ⓐ 9   Ⓑ 20   Ⓒ 5   Ⓓ 10

4. $\frac{1}{8}$ and $\frac{2}{6}$

    Ⓐ 8   Ⓑ 16   Ⓒ 48   Ⓓ 24

5. $\frac{1}{3}$ and $\frac{3}{9}$

    Ⓐ 12   Ⓑ 15   Ⓒ 18   Ⓓ 9

6. $\frac{1}{9}$ and $\frac{3}{6}$

    Ⓐ 12   Ⓑ 15   Ⓒ 18   Ⓓ 9

Directions: Add or subtract these fractions and mixed numbers. Reduce answers to lowest terms.

7. $\frac{1}{4} + \frac{2}{3} =$

    Ⓐ $\frac{3}{7}$ Ⓑ $\frac{11}{12}$ Ⓒ $\frac{8}{12}$ Ⓓ $\frac{5}{12}$

8. $\frac{4}{5} - \frac{2}{4} =$

    Ⓐ $\frac{1}{5}$ Ⓑ $\frac{3}{10}$ Ⓒ $\frac{3}{5}$ Ⓓ $\frac{2}{9}$

9. $\frac{9}{10} - \frac{2}{5} =$

    Ⓐ $\frac{1}{2}$ Ⓑ $\frac{7}{10}$ Ⓒ $\frac{5}{5}$ Ⓓ $\frac{4}{10}$

10. $\frac{7}{8} - \frac{1}{6} =$

    Ⓐ $\frac{17}{24}$ Ⓑ $\frac{5}{8}$ Ⓒ $\frac{6}{12}$ Ⓓ $\frac{19}{24}$

11. $\frac{2}{3} - \frac{2}{7} =$

    Ⓐ $\frac{8}{12}$ Ⓑ $\frac{9}{21}$ Ⓒ $\frac{8}{21}$ Ⓓ $\frac{4}{10}$

12. $\frac{4}{7} - \frac{2}{5} =$

    Ⓐ $\frac{6}{35}$ Ⓑ $\frac{1}{3}$ Ⓒ $\frac{34}{35}$ Ⓓ $\frac{2}{12}$

13. $\frac{9}{12} + \frac{1}{6} =$

    Ⓐ $1\frac{1}{2}$ Ⓑ $\frac{11}{18}$ Ⓒ $\frac{11}{12}$ Ⓓ $\frac{4}{15}$

14. $\frac{11}{15} - \frac{3}{5} =$

    Ⓐ $\frac{3}{15}$ Ⓑ $\frac{11}{30}$ Ⓒ $\frac{2}{30}$ Ⓓ $\frac{2}{15}$

15. $1\frac{2}{3} + 2\frac{1}{4} =$

    Ⓐ $3\frac{11}{12}$ Ⓑ $4\frac{5}{12}$ Ⓒ $1\frac{11}{12}$ Ⓓ $3\frac{3}{7}$

16. $3\frac{1}{2} - 1\frac{1}{3} =$

    Ⓐ $2\frac{1}{6}$ Ⓑ $2\frac{2}{3}$ Ⓒ $4\frac{5}{6}$ Ⓓ $\frac{2}{15}$

Test Practice 3

Directions: Multiply and divide these fractions. Simplify answers to lowest terms.

1. $\frac{3}{4} \times 12 =$
Ⓐ 8   Ⓑ 9   Ⓒ $3\frac{3}{4}$ Ⓓ $\frac{12}{3}$

2. $9 \times \frac{2}{3} =$
Ⓐ 6   Ⓑ $\frac{18}{27}$ Ⓒ 8   Ⓓ $1\frac{2}{3}$

3. $\frac{1}{2} \times 24 =$
Ⓐ 10   Ⓑ $12\frac{1}{2}$ Ⓒ 12   Ⓓ $\frac{1}{48}$

4. $25 \times \frac{3}{5} =$
Ⓐ 15   Ⓑ 18   Ⓒ $\frac{75}{25}$ Ⓓ 9

5. $\frac{5}{6}$ of 12 =
Ⓐ 11   Ⓑ 10   Ⓒ 14   Ⓓ $10\frac{1}{2}$

6. $\frac{1}{4}$ of 16 =
Ⓐ 8   Ⓑ $7\frac{1}{2}$ Ⓒ 4   Ⓓ $8\frac{1}{2}$

7. $\frac{1}{3} \times \frac{5}{6} =$
Ⓐ $\frac{5}{9}$ Ⓑ $\frac{5}{18}$ Ⓒ $\frac{5}{9}$ Ⓓ $\frac{11}{16}$

8. $\frac{1}{8} \times \frac{2}{3} =$
Ⓐ $\frac{2}{22}$ Ⓑ $1\frac{1}{12}$ Ⓒ $\frac{1}{12}$ Ⓓ $\frac{3}{24}$

9. $\frac{4}{7} \times \frac{1}{3} =$
Ⓐ $\frac{21}{4}$ Ⓑ $2\frac{1}{4}$ Ⓒ $\frac{4}{21}$ Ⓓ $\frac{5}{21}$

10. $\frac{3}{5} \times \frac{3}{4} =$
Ⓐ $\frac{9}{20}$ Ⓑ $\frac{3}{4}$ Ⓒ $\frac{12}{15}$ Ⓓ $1\frac{1}{9}$

11. $\frac{2}{3} \div \frac{1}{4} =$
Ⓐ $\frac{2}{12}$ Ⓑ $3\frac{2}{3}$ Ⓒ $2\frac{2}{3}$ Ⓓ 6

12. $\frac{3}{5} \div \frac{1}{2} =$
Ⓐ $\frac{4}{5}$ Ⓑ $\frac{7}{5}$ Ⓒ $1\frac{3}{10}$ Ⓓ $1\frac{1}{5}$

13. $\frac{6}{8} \div \frac{1}{4} =$
Ⓐ $3\frac{1}{24}$ Ⓑ 3   Ⓒ 2   Ⓓ $\frac{6}{32}$

14. $\frac{5}{12} \div \frac{1}{3} =$
Ⓐ $1\frac{5}{12}$ Ⓑ $1\frac{1}{4}$ Ⓒ $\frac{36}{5}$ Ⓓ $1\frac{3}{4}$

15. $9 \div \frac{1}{3} =$
Ⓐ 27   Ⓑ 3   Ⓒ 18   Ⓓ $3\frac{1}{3}$

16. $12 \div \frac{1}{2} =$
Ⓐ 6   Ⓑ $2\frac{1}{4}$ Ⓒ 24   Ⓓ $6\frac{1}{2}$

Directions: Convert these fractions to decimals.

17. $\frac{1}{2} =$
Ⓐ 0.12   Ⓑ 0.05   Ⓒ 0.5   Ⓓ 0.25

18. $\frac{1}{4} =$
Ⓐ 0.33   Ⓑ 0.14   Ⓒ 0.025   Ⓓ 0.25

19. $\frac{4}{5} =$
Ⓐ 0.45   Ⓑ 0.8   Ⓒ 0.08   Ⓓ 0.6

20. $\frac{3}{8} =$
Ⓐ 0.375   Ⓑ 0.357   Ⓒ 0.035   Ⓓ 0.24

21. $\frac{9}{10} =$
Ⓐ 0.9   Ⓑ 0.09   Ⓒ 0.99   Ⓓ 0.910

22. $\frac{5}{6} =$
Ⓐ 0.823   Ⓑ 0.567   Ⓒ 0.833   Ⓓ 0.85

Test Practice 4

Directions: Choose the decimal with the greatest value.

1. Ⓐ 0.25 Ⓑ 0.51 Ⓒ 0.5 Ⓓ 0.256 | 2. Ⓐ 0.006 Ⓑ 0.60 Ⓒ 0.7 Ⓓ 0.556

3. Ⓐ 2.678 Ⓑ 2.7 Ⓒ 2.1113 Ⓓ 3.1 | 4. Ⓐ 0.09 Ⓑ 0.18 Ⓒ 0.2 Ⓓ 0.009

5. Ⓐ 0.005 Ⓑ 0.5 Ⓒ 0.501 Ⓓ 0.05 | 6. Ⓐ 2.0 Ⓑ 1.987 Ⓒ 0.999 Ⓓ 2.1

Directions: Compute the sums and differences of these decimals.

7. 4.1 + 0.334 =
   Ⓐ 4.424 Ⓑ 7.44 Ⓒ 4.434 Ⓓ 3.834

8. 8.09 − 7.619 =
   Ⓐ 15.628 Ⓑ 0.471 Ⓒ 1.610 Ⓓ 1.471

9. 8.3 + 10 =
   Ⓐ 13.8 Ⓑ 18.3 Ⓒ 9.4 Ⓓ 18.7

10. 7 − 0.234 =
    Ⓐ 7.234 Ⓑ 6.234 Ⓒ 6.676 Ⓓ 6.766

11. 17.03 − 14.003 =
    Ⓐ 3.27 Ⓑ 3.027 Ⓒ 31.033 Ⓓ 31.027

12. 0.1 − 0.0236 =
    Ⓐ 0.0764 Ⓑ 0.00764 Ⓒ 1.746 Ⓓ 0.1236

13. 4.01 − 3.987 =
    Ⓐ 0.0023 Ⓑ 0.23 Ⓒ 23 Ⓓ 0.023

14. 1 − 0.111 =
    Ⓐ 0.889 Ⓑ 0.899 Ⓒ 0.0889 Ⓓ 1.111

15. 6.444 + 4.666 =
    Ⓐ 1.778 Ⓑ 10.11 Ⓒ 111.1 Ⓓ 11.11

16. 9 − 8.119 =
    Ⓐ 0.881 Ⓑ 0.0881 Ⓒ 17.119 Ⓓ 1.119

17. 80 − 0.1111 =
    Ⓐ 79.8889 Ⓑ 69.8889 Ⓒ 80.1111 Ⓓ 79.8999

18. 0.025 + 2.5 =
    Ⓐ 2.525 Ⓑ 2.552 Ⓒ 5.0 Ⓓ 2.535

19. 11 − 10.999 =
    Ⓐ 0.0001 Ⓑ 0.1 Ⓒ 0.011 Ⓓ 0.001

20. 5 − 0.0006 =
    Ⓐ 4.999 Ⓑ 5.0004 Ⓒ 4.9499 Ⓓ 4.9994

21. 1.0 + 0.11 =
    Ⓐ 0.111 Ⓑ 11.1 Ⓒ 0.89 Ⓓ 1.11

22. 2 − 0.002 =
    Ⓐ 1.998 Ⓑ 1.9089 Ⓒ 0.998 Ⓓ 2.002

Test Practice 5

Directions: Multiply and divide these decimals as indicated. Show your work on a separate sheet of paper.

1. 2.23 x 10 =

(A) 22.3 (B) 2.23 (C) 0.23 (D) 223

2. 0.4633 x 10 =

(A) 4.633 (B) 46.33 (C) 4,633 (D) 463.3

3. 100 x 0.15 =

(A) 0.1500 (B) 1.5 (C) 15.00 (D) 0.0015

4. 0.169 x 100 =

(A) 169.0 (B) 0.00169 (C) 16.9 (D) 1.69

5. 4.458 x 1,000 =

(A) 4,458 (B) 44.58 (C) 0.04458 (D) 445.8

6. 0.7437 x 1,000 =

(A) 74.37 (B) 743.7 (C) 0.007437 (D) 7437.0

7. 9.8 x 0.5 =

(A) 4.9 (B) 49.0 (C) 0.049 (D) 490.0

8. 1.2 x 4.3 =

(A) 51.6 (B) 516.0 (C) 0.0516 (D) 5.16

9. 0.09 x 0.008 =

(A) 0.72 (B) 0.00072 (C) 0.0072 (D) 72.0

10. 0.0004 x 0.120 =

(A) 480.0 (B) 0.00048 (C) 4.8 (D) 0.000048

11. 7.9 x 4 =

(A) 31.6 (B) 316.0 (C) 0.316 (D) 3.16

12. 5.8 x 60 =

(A) 348 (B) 3.48 (C) 0.0348 (D) 34.8

13. $6\overline{)60.6}$

(A) 1.01 (B) 101.0 (C) 100.1 (D) 10.1

14. $5\overline{)20.50}$

(A) 4.01 (B) 4.10 (C) 401.0 (D) 4.11

15. $9\overline{)3.681}$

(A) 0.409 (B) 4.09 (C) 409.0 (D) 40.90

16. $20\overline{)406.0}$

(A) 203.0 (B) 2.03 (C) 20.3 (D) 0.203

17. $.03\overline{)609.03}$

(A) 203.01 (B) 2,030.1 (C) 20.301 (D) 20,301.0

18. $.07\overline{)21.07}$

(A) 3.01 (B) 3,010.0 (C) 301.0 (D) 0.301

19. $.007\overline{)21.14}$

(A) 30.2 (B) 0.302 (C) 3,020.0 (D) 302.0

20. $.018\overline{)90.36}$

(A) 5,020.0 (B) 5.020 (C) 0.5020 (D) 502.0

21. $8\overline{)5.0}$

(A) 0.625 (B) 62.5 (C) 6.25 (D) 0.0625

22. $.08\overline{)6}$

(A) 0.075 (B) 0.75 (C) 7.50 (D) 75.0

Test Practice 6   ✺   ✺   ✺   ✺   ✺   ✺   ✺   ✺

Directions: Convert these decimals and fractions to percents.

1. 0.25 =

    (A) 25%   (B) 2.5%   (C) 0.25%   (D) 0.025%

2. 0.33 =

    (A) 3.3%   (B) 0.33%   (C) 330%   (D) 33%

3. 0.81 =

    (A) 81%   (B) 8.1%   (C) 0.81%   (D) 810%

4. 0.03 =

    (A) 30%   (B) 3%   (C) 0.03%   (D) 0.3%

5. $\frac{1}{2}$ =

    (A) 5%   (B) 50%   (C) 0.5%   (D) 500%

6. $\frac{1}{4}$ =

    (A) 0.25%   (B) 25%   (C) 0.025%   (D) 2.5%

7. $\frac{2}{3}$ =

    (A) 6.7%   (B) 0.67%   (C) 67%   (D) 670%

8. $\frac{6}{10}$ =

    (A) 60%   (B) 6%   (C) 0.60%   (D) 0.06%

Directions: Compute these discounts, sale prices, and interest charges.

9. 10% discount on a $300 TV

    (A) $30 off   (B) $13 off
    (C) $3 off   (D) $0.30 off

10. 15% discount on $40 shoes

    (A) $16 off   (B) $10 off
    (C) $26 off   (D) $6 off

11. 12% discount on a $25 pizza

    (A) $6 off   (B) $5 off
    (C) $3 off   (D) $9 off

12. 24% discount on a $100 show ticket

    (A) $24 off   (B) $12 off
    (C) $42 off   (D) $20 off

13. 20%-off sale — $80 coat

    (A) $61 final cost   (B) $64 final cost
    (C) $65 final cost   (D) $66 final cost

14. 22%-off sale — $70 shoes

    (A) $56.40 final cost   (B) $58.60 final cost
    (C) $54.60 final cost   (D) $58.40 final cost

15. 20%-off sale — $12.50 watch

    (A) $9.00 final cost   (B) $10.00 final cost
    (C) $11.00 final cost   (D) $12.00 final cost

16. 18%-off sale — $203 bicycle

    (A) $167.46 final cost   (B) $166.46 final cost
    (C) $167.64 final cost   (D) $166.64 final cost

17. $1,000 loan for 1 year; 20% interest

    (A) $2.00   (B) $20   (C) $2,000   (D) $200

18. $400 loan for 3 years; 23% interest

    (A) $276   (B) $92   (C) $27.60   (D) $920

19. $4,000 loan for 5 years; 27% interest

    (A) $540   (B) $5.40   (C) $54.00   (D) $5,400

20. $100 loan for 2 years; 12% interest

    (A) $2.40   (B) $240   (C) $0.24   (D) $24

Answer Sheet

Test Practice 1
1. Ⓐ Ⓑ Ⓒ Ⓓ
2. Ⓐ Ⓑ Ⓒ Ⓓ
3. Ⓐ Ⓑ Ⓒ Ⓓ
4. Ⓐ Ⓑ Ⓒ Ⓓ
5. Ⓐ Ⓑ Ⓒ Ⓓ
6. Ⓐ Ⓑ Ⓒ Ⓓ
7. Ⓐ Ⓑ Ⓒ Ⓓ
8. Ⓐ Ⓑ Ⓒ Ⓓ
9. Ⓐ Ⓑ Ⓒ Ⓓ
10. Ⓐ Ⓑ Ⓒ Ⓓ
11. Ⓐ Ⓑ Ⓒ Ⓓ
12. Ⓐ Ⓑ Ⓒ Ⓓ
13. Ⓐ Ⓑ Ⓒ Ⓓ
14. Ⓐ Ⓑ Ⓒ Ⓓ
15. Ⓐ Ⓑ Ⓒ Ⓓ
16. Ⓐ Ⓑ Ⓒ Ⓓ
17. Ⓐ Ⓑ Ⓒ Ⓓ
18. Ⓐ Ⓑ Ⓒ Ⓓ
19. Ⓐ Ⓑ Ⓒ Ⓓ
20. Ⓐ Ⓑ Ⓒ Ⓓ

Test Practice 2
1. Ⓐ Ⓑ Ⓒ Ⓓ
2. Ⓐ Ⓑ Ⓒ Ⓓ
3. Ⓐ Ⓑ Ⓒ Ⓓ
4. Ⓐ Ⓑ Ⓒ Ⓓ
5. Ⓐ Ⓑ Ⓒ Ⓓ
6. Ⓐ Ⓑ Ⓒ Ⓓ
7. Ⓐ Ⓑ Ⓒ Ⓓ
8. Ⓐ Ⓑ Ⓒ Ⓓ
9. Ⓐ Ⓑ Ⓒ Ⓓ
10. Ⓐ Ⓑ Ⓒ Ⓓ
11. Ⓐ Ⓑ Ⓒ Ⓓ
12. Ⓐ Ⓑ Ⓒ Ⓓ
13. Ⓐ Ⓑ Ⓒ Ⓓ
14. Ⓐ Ⓑ Ⓒ Ⓓ
15. Ⓐ Ⓑ Ⓒ Ⓓ
16. Ⓐ Ⓑ Ⓒ Ⓓ

Test Practice 3
1. Ⓐ Ⓑ Ⓒ Ⓓ
2. Ⓐ Ⓑ Ⓒ Ⓓ
3. Ⓐ Ⓑ Ⓒ Ⓓ
4. Ⓐ Ⓑ Ⓒ Ⓓ
5. Ⓐ Ⓑ Ⓒ Ⓓ
6. Ⓐ Ⓑ Ⓒ Ⓓ
7. Ⓐ Ⓑ Ⓒ Ⓓ
8. Ⓐ Ⓑ Ⓒ Ⓓ
9. Ⓐ Ⓑ Ⓒ Ⓓ
10. Ⓐ Ⓑ Ⓒ Ⓓ
11. Ⓐ Ⓑ Ⓒ Ⓓ
12. Ⓐ Ⓑ Ⓒ Ⓓ
13. Ⓐ Ⓑ Ⓒ Ⓓ
14. Ⓐ Ⓑ Ⓒ Ⓓ
15. Ⓐ Ⓑ Ⓒ Ⓓ
16. Ⓐ Ⓑ Ⓒ Ⓓ
17. Ⓐ Ⓑ Ⓒ Ⓓ
18. Ⓐ Ⓑ Ⓒ Ⓓ
19. Ⓐ Ⓑ Ⓒ Ⓓ
20. Ⓐ Ⓑ Ⓒ Ⓓ
21. Ⓐ Ⓑ Ⓒ Ⓓ
22. Ⓐ Ⓑ Ⓒ Ⓓ

Test Practice 4
1. Ⓐ Ⓑ Ⓒ Ⓓ
2. Ⓐ Ⓑ Ⓒ Ⓓ
3. Ⓐ Ⓑ Ⓒ Ⓓ
4. Ⓐ Ⓑ Ⓒ Ⓓ
5. Ⓐ Ⓑ Ⓒ Ⓓ
6. Ⓐ Ⓑ Ⓒ Ⓓ
7. Ⓐ Ⓑ Ⓒ Ⓓ
8. Ⓐ Ⓑ Ⓒ Ⓓ
9. Ⓐ Ⓑ Ⓒ Ⓓ
10. Ⓐ Ⓑ Ⓒ Ⓓ
11. Ⓐ Ⓑ Ⓒ Ⓓ
12. Ⓐ Ⓑ Ⓒ Ⓓ
13. Ⓐ Ⓑ Ⓒ Ⓓ
14. Ⓐ Ⓑ Ⓒ Ⓓ
15. Ⓐ Ⓑ Ⓒ Ⓓ
16. Ⓐ Ⓑ Ⓒ Ⓓ
17. Ⓐ Ⓑ Ⓒ Ⓓ
18. Ⓐ Ⓑ Ⓒ Ⓓ
19. Ⓐ Ⓑ Ⓒ Ⓓ
20. Ⓐ Ⓑ Ⓒ Ⓓ
21. Ⓐ Ⓑ Ⓒ Ⓓ
22. Ⓐ Ⓑ Ⓒ Ⓓ

Test Practice 5
1. Ⓐ Ⓑ Ⓒ Ⓓ
2. Ⓐ Ⓑ Ⓒ Ⓓ
3. Ⓐ Ⓑ Ⓒ Ⓓ
4. Ⓐ Ⓑ Ⓒ Ⓓ
5. Ⓐ Ⓑ Ⓒ Ⓓ
6. Ⓐ Ⓑ Ⓒ Ⓓ
7. Ⓐ Ⓑ Ⓒ Ⓓ
8. Ⓐ Ⓑ Ⓒ Ⓓ
9. Ⓐ Ⓑ Ⓒ Ⓓ
10. Ⓐ Ⓑ Ⓒ Ⓓ
11. Ⓐ Ⓑ Ⓒ Ⓓ
12. Ⓐ Ⓑ Ⓒ Ⓓ
13. Ⓐ Ⓑ Ⓒ Ⓓ
14. Ⓐ Ⓑ Ⓒ Ⓓ
15. Ⓐ Ⓑ Ⓒ Ⓓ
16. Ⓐ Ⓑ Ⓒ Ⓓ
17. Ⓐ Ⓑ Ⓒ Ⓓ
18. Ⓐ Ⓑ Ⓒ Ⓓ
19. Ⓐ Ⓑ Ⓒ Ⓓ
20. Ⓐ Ⓑ Ⓒ Ⓓ
21. Ⓐ Ⓑ Ⓒ Ⓓ
22. Ⓐ Ⓑ Ⓒ Ⓓ

Test Practice 6
1. Ⓐ Ⓑ Ⓒ Ⓓ
2. Ⓐ Ⓑ Ⓒ Ⓓ
3. Ⓐ Ⓑ Ⓒ Ⓓ
4. Ⓐ Ⓑ Ⓒ Ⓓ
5. Ⓐ Ⓑ Ⓒ Ⓓ
6. Ⓐ Ⓑ Ⓒ Ⓓ
7. Ⓐ Ⓑ Ⓒ Ⓓ
8. Ⓐ Ⓑ Ⓒ Ⓓ
9. Ⓐ Ⓑ Ⓒ Ⓓ
10. Ⓐ Ⓑ Ⓒ Ⓓ
11. Ⓐ Ⓑ Ⓒ Ⓓ
12. Ⓐ Ⓑ Ⓒ Ⓓ
13. Ⓐ Ⓑ Ⓒ Ⓓ
14. Ⓐ Ⓑ Ⓒ Ⓓ
15. Ⓐ Ⓑ Ⓒ Ⓓ
16. Ⓐ Ⓑ Ⓒ Ⓓ
17. Ⓐ Ⓑ Ⓒ Ⓓ
18. Ⓐ Ⓑ Ⓒ Ⓓ
19. Ⓐ Ⓑ Ⓒ Ⓓ
20. Ⓐ Ⓑ Ⓒ Ⓓ

Answer Key

Practice 1
1. 1/2
2. 1/4
3. 3/10
4. 1/6
5. 2/5
6. 5/8
7. 2/7
8. 2/6 = 1/3
9. 5/9
10. 3/6 = 1/2
11. 1/8
12. 4/4 = 1
13. 2/4 = 1/2
14. 1/3
15. 1/2
16. 4/7
17. 3/12 = 1/4
18. 5/9
19. 9/18 = 1/2
20. 5/12
21. 3/10
22. 3/3 = 1
23. 13/20
24. 3/4

Practice 2
1. 2/4
2. 2/3
3. 2/16
4. 6/8
5. 8/10
6. 6/10
7. 1/3
8. 3/4
9. 6/16
10. 1/2
11. 5/6
12. 1/2
13. 12/12
14. 21/24
15. 10/18
16. 6/6
17. 12/12
18. 20/20
19. 4/14
20. 16/20
21. 6/24
22. 3/9
23. 2/8
24. 8/24
25. 12/15
26. 8/24
27. 8/18

Practice 3
1. 2; 2/3
2. 5; 1/2
3. 7; 1/3
4. 2; 7/8
5. 5; 1/3
6. 2; 1/4
7. 12; 1/2
8. 5; 1/5
9. 3; 2/3
10. 7; 1/2
11. 25; 1/2
12. 5, 3/5
13. 9; 1/2
14. 3; 3/5
15. 11; 2/3
16. 7; 2/3
17. 6; 2/3
18. 4; 5/6
19. 3; 9/11
20. 6; 5/6
21. 10; 4/5
22. 6; 3/4
23. 8; 2/3
24. 9; 2/3

Practice 4
1. 1 1/2
2. 1 1/4
3. 1 1/5
4. 1 1/6
5. 2 1/4
6. 1 4/5
7. 1 9/10
8. 1 5/7
9. 2 5/6
10. 3
11. 4
12. 3
13. 2
14. 5
15. 4
16. 11/3
17. 14/3
18. 13/2
19. 11/2
20. 9/4
21. 21/5
22. 10/3
23. 11/4
24. 22/3
25. 9/2
26. 13/6
27. 11/2
28. 19/4
29. 15/4
30. 13/12

Practice 5
1. <
2. <
3. <
4. <
5. >
6. >
7. <
8. >
9. >
10. <
11. <
12. <
13. <
14. <
15. >
16. >
17. >
18. <

Practice 6
1. >
2. =
3. <
4. <
5. >
6. >
7. =
8. <
9. <
10. <
11. =
12. <
13. <
14. >
15. <
16. >
17. >
18. >
19. <
20. >
21. >
22. <
23. <
24. >

Practice 7
1. 5/8, 3/4, 1 1/2
2. 4/12, 1 1/3, 1 3/6
3. 3/9, 1/2, 4/3
4. 5/6, 9/8, 1 3/4
5. 4/6, 9/8, 2 1/2
6. 3/12, 4/3, 1 7/8
7. 5/12, 7/8, 7/5
8. 3/4, 5/6, 11/6
9. 7/8, 3/2, 2 1/4
10. 3/9, 1/2, 6/3
11. 1/4, 9/10, 1 1/2
12. 3/4, 4/3, 3 1/2
13. 1/2, 5/8, 2/1
14. 3/4, 4/2, 2 1/2
15. 3/6, 7/12, 5/3
16. 6/12, 6/4, 1 3/4
17. 4/6, 1 1/3, 3/2
18. 4/12, 1 2/3, 9/3
19. 1/6, 2 1/3, 6/2
20. 3/2, 1 5/8, 2/1
21. 7/4, 1 7/8, 12/6
22. 3/4, 8/6, 1 4/8
23. 2/3, 9/4, 3 1/4
24. 10/12, 2 1/3, 7/2

Practice 8
1. 15
2. 24
3. 12
4. 12
5. 30
6. 14
7. 24
8. 6
9. 8
10. 9
11. 18
12. 40
13. 10
14. 60
15. 36
16. 18
17. 40
18. 21
19. 30
20. 16
21. 27

Practice 9
1. 3/4
2. 1/4
3. 3/6 = 1/2
4. 1/8
5. 5/10 = 1/2
6. 6/9 = 2/3
7. 19/20
8. 9/12 = 3/4
9. 7/10
10. 4/20 = 1/5
11. 14/24 = 7/12
12. 5/24
13. 4/15
14. 40/33 = 1 7/33
15. 9/24 = 3/8
16. 13/36
17. 16/12 = 1 4/12 = 1 1/3
18. 6/12 = 1/2
19. 1/10
20. 7/18
21. 19/36
22. 26/24 = 1 2/24 = 1 1/12
23. 31/35
24. 6/40 = 3/20
25. 1/8
26. 7/15

Practice 10
1. 1 5/12
2. 6 23/24
3. 5 5/6
4. 3 7/10
5. 6 3/4
6. 4 1/9
7. 4 1/8
8. 5 3/8
9. 8 17/24
10. 5 1/8
11. 4 11/28
12. 3 5/6
13. 5 5/12
14. 6 5/12
15. 9 5/6
16. 4 5/6
17. 2 3/10
18. 5 3/8

Practice 11
1. 5 7/6 = 6 1/6
2. 5 9/8 = 6 1/8
3. 9 12/12 = 10
4. 6 7/6 = 7 1/6
5. 5 11/10 = 6 1/10
6. 3 5/4 = 4 1/4
7. 6 14/9 = 7 5/9
8. 9 17/12 = 10 5/12
9. 2 5/6
10. 3 3/4
11. 2 19/24
12. 2 3/6 = 2 1/2
13. 2 13/15
14. 4/12 = 1/3
15. 5/12
16. 5 7/12

Practice 12
1. 1 1/8
2. 5 3/9 = 5 1/3
3. 2
4. 2 1/7
5. 2 2/5
6. 1 4/6 = 1 2/3
7. 16
8. 3 6/12 = 3 1/2
9. 1 7/8
10. 9
11. 1 1/4
12. 15
13. 9
14. 2 1/10
15. 7 4/8 = 7 1/2
16. 2
17. 10
18. 12
19. 2
20. 3
21. 9
22. 16
23. 6
24. 20
25. 7
26. 10
27. 6
28. 3 3/4

Practice 13
1. 1/3
2. 3/5
3. 3/4
4. 1/6
5. 1/2
6. 1/3
7. 2/5
8. 2/5
9. 2/5
10. 1/9
11. 1/3
12. 3/2 = 1 1/2
13. 1/13
14. 1/8
15. 1
16. 2/7
17. 6/35
18. 3/11
19. 4/9
20. 3/10
21. 9/40
22. 18/35
23. 1/20
24. 3/8

Practice 14
1. 1 1/3
2. 2 1/4
3. 1 2/10 = 1 1/5
4. 20/5 = 4
5. 21/7 = 3
6. 4/5
7. 6/6 = 1
8. 8/8 = 1
9. 12/12 = 1
10. 1/16
11. 4/49
12. 25/81
13. 18/4 = 4 2/4 = 4 1/2
14. 10/64 = 5/32
15. 14/18 = 7/9
16. 16/12 = 1 4/12 = 1 1/3
17. 8/24 = 1/3
18. 8/40 = 1/5
19. 6/9 = 2/3
20. 28/20 = 1 8/20 = 1 2/5
21. 42/42 = 1
22. 16/12 = 1 4/12 = 1 1/3
23. 24/4 = 6
24. 9/15 = 3/5
25. 3/2 = 1 1/2
26. 2/4 = 1/2
27. 3/8
28. 32/36 = 8/9

Practice 15
1. 5
2. 2
3. 8
4. 4
5. 4
6. 5
7. 3
8. 2
9. 8
10. 5
11. 7
12. 2
13. 21
14. 4
15. 7
16. 5
17. 3
18. 8
19. 2
20. 1
21. 1
22. 5
23. 4
24. 3

Practice 16
1. 0.75
2. 0.125
3. 0.5
4. 0.875
5. 0.8
6. 0.5
7. 0.7
8. 0.2
9. 0.333
10. 0.4
11. 0.65
12. 0.5
13. 0.666
14. 0.75
15. 0.833
16. 0.111
17. 0.444
18. 0.375
19. 0.142
20. 0.083

Practice 17
1. 3/10
2. 1 4/100
3. 1 6/100
4. 5/1000
5. 9/10
6. 8/1000
7. 1 25/100
8. 7/1000
9. 1 34/100
10. 3 4/1000
11. 4 6/100
12. 1 98/1000
13. 3 25/100
14. 4 7/1000
15. 3 19/1000
16. 1 1/1000
17. 1 1/10
18. 1 11/100
19. 1 111/1000
20. 2 2/100
21. 3 31/1000
22. 23 5/1000
23. 16 4/1000
24. 36 7/1000
25. 11 678/1000
26. 22 234/1000
27. 33 509/1000
28. 14/1000
29. 777/1000
30. 1 71/1000
31. 4 4/1000
32. 405/1000
33. 8 88/1000

Practice 18
1. forty-five thousandths
2. twenty-three and twelve hundredths
3. four hundred fifteen thousandths
4. three hundredths
5. thirty-four hundredths
6. sixteen hundredths
7. three and five thousandths
8. one and nine hundredths
9. two and seven thousandths
10. two and eight hundredths
11. forty-one and fourteen hundredths
12. seven and eighty-one thousandths
13. four and one thousandth
14. two and one hundred one thousandths
15. five and one hundred thirty-two thousandths
16. three and twenty-six thousandths
17. five and one hundred ten thousandths
18. nineteen and six thousandths
19. one and twenty thousandths
20. nine and ninety-nine hundredths
21. nine and nine hundred ninety-nine thousandths
22. nine and nine hundred nine thousandths
23. four and two hundred three thousandths
24. six and six hundred sixty-six thousandths

Answer Key

Practice 19
1. >	10. <	19. <	28. >
2. <	11. <	20. <	29. >
3. <	12. <	21. <	30. <
4. >	13. <	22. <	31. <
5. <	14. >	23. <	32. >
6. <	15. >	24. <	33. >
7. <	16. >	25. <	
8. <	17. >	26. >	
9. <	18. <	27. <	

Practice 20
1. 0.06, 0.25, 0.30
2. 0.50, 0.65, 0.90
3. 0.10, 0.2, 0.35
4. 0.09, 0.9, 1.95
5. 0.06, 0.60, 1.05
6. 0.24, 1.04, 2.4
7. 1.6, 1.61, 2
8. 1.05, 1.50, 2.5
9. 0.7, 0.79, 0.8
10. 1.02, 1.2, 2.01
11. 1.03, 1.43, 1.5
12. 2.0, 2.01, 2.1
13. 3.04, 3.111, 3.4
14. 4.44, 5.033, 5.5
15. 0.11, 1.013, 1.101
16. 6.031, 6.6, 6.66
17. 6.999, 7.1, 7.17
18. 4.9, 5.051, 5.15
19. 1.18, 1.8, 1.810
20. 1.34, 3.101, 3.313
21. 3.011, 3.101, 3.11
22. 0.412, 1.041, 1.411
23. 5.5, 5.505, 5.55
24. 1.244, 3.214, 3.3
25. 1.134, 3.3, 3.41
26. 5.999, 6.701, 7.1
27. 0.003, 3.303, 3.31
28. 2.9, 3.001, 3.101
29. 5.946, 5.947, 5.95
30. 5.9, 6.001, 6.17

Practice 21
1. 11.021	10. 9.09	19. 15.097
2. 6.183	11. 6.606	20. 40.101
3. 1.231	12. 19.000	21. 2.11
4. 19.021	13. 12.106	22. 2.812
5. 1.012	14. 1.903	23. 1.811
6. 26.401	15. 16.788	24. 7.606
7. 7.014	16. 0.715	25. 7.01
8. 10.699	17. 2.079	26. 18.2
9. 100.608	18. 6.108	27. 50.2

Practice 22
1. 4.266	10. 1.899	19. 1.871
2. 0.087	11. 3.781	20. 6.998
3. 4.44	12. 0.812	21. 2.969
4. 11.268	13. 1.02	22. 4.579
5. 6.713	14. 1.23	23. 29.178
6. 5.398	15. 0.113	24. 1.09
7. 0.089	16. 1.997	25. 1.32
8. 3.287	17. 6.992	26. 3.029
9. 1.781	18. 28.922	27. 12.987

Practice 23
1. 34	13. 60	25. 5,555
2. 280	14. 1.12	26. 8.8
3. 4,500	15. 1,120	27. 341.4
4. 57	16. 1,122	28. 30.1
5. 96	17. 213	29. 20
6. 140	18. 32,300	30. 30
7. 51	19. 0.01	31. 14
8. 23	20. 0.1	32. 24.5
9. 1	21. 1	33. 150
10. 20	22. 200	34. 1,100
11. 9	23. 77.7	35. 2,810
12. 5	24. 6,660	36. 2,995

Practice 24
1. 2.31	9. 0.2177916	17. 0.00186
2. 0.00869	10. 8.73152	18. 66,022.0
3. 0.0552	11. 0.3075	19. 0.6885
4. 14.08	12. 3,471.6	20. 2,589.168
5. 0.003924	13. 34.50	21. 35,566.620
6. 0.2970	14. 18.9999	22. 0.00072
7. 0.2211	15. 56.78	23. 6.73569
8. 5.377260	16. 39.40	24. 2,314.92

Practice 25
1. 0.54	10. 88.91	19. 0.778
2. 0.0378	11. 0.041	20. 0.003
3. 0.0009	12. 0.045	21. 234.5
4. 0.678	13. 0.44	22. 0.20
5. 0.0089	14. 0.886	23. 0.05
6. 0.00078	15. 35.4	24. 3.145
7. 0.6701	16. 0.56	25. 0.1
8. 0.054	17. 0.5	26. 0.01
9. 0.161	18. 0.456	27. 0.1

Practice 26
1. 1.06	8. 1.206	15. 0.305
2. 4.22	9. 1.5	16. 0.409
3. 7.02	10. 8.55	17. 0.05
4. 0.12	11. 0.85	18. 1.62
5. 7.04	12. 0.302	19. 0.302
6. 1.1	13. 1.05	20. 0.302
7. 0.13	14. 0.64	21. 0.605

Practice 27
1. 81	7. 300	13. 2,400
2. 201	8. 304	14. 11,000
3. 4.05	9. 20.1	15. 200,000
4. 20	10. 2.09	16. 300
5. 2.04	11. 20	17. 300
6. 21	12. 21,000	18. 22

Practice 28
1. 0.66 - repeating
2. 2.10 - terminating
3. 0.333 - repeating
4. 0.625 - terminating
5. 0.444 - repeating
6. 0.75 - terminating
7. 0.777 - repeating
8. 0.888 - repeating
9. 0.8333 - repeating
10. terminating
11. terminating
12. repeating
13. repeating
14. irrational
15. repeating
16. irrational
17. repeating

Practice 29
1. 10%	7. 1%	13. 50%
2. 25%	8. 12%	14. 18%
3. 3%	9. 66%	15. 31%
4. 16%	10. 75%	16. 6%
5. 88%	11. 90%	17. 29%
6. 99%	12. 40%	18. 79%

Practice 30
1. 35%	12. 239%	23. 0.9013
2. 402%	13. 0.5%	24. 0.064
3. 4%	14. 1.2%	25. 0.44
4. 2%	15. 900.3%	26. 0.194
5. 91%	16. 101%	27. 0.011
6. 107%	17. 300.1%	28. 0.0113
7. 109%	18. 770%	29. 0.04
8. 8%	19. 0.24	30. 0.825
9. 1706%	20. 0.023	31. 0.07
10. 13%	21. 0.0908	32. 0.0103
11. 1%	22. 0.034	33. 0.01

Practice 31
1. 0.50 = 50%
2. 0.285 = 28.5%
3. 0.50 = 50%
4. 0.75 = 75%
5. 0.625 = 62.5%
6. 0.40 = 40%
7. 0.777 = 77.7% or 77.8%
8. 0.60 = 60%
9. 0.25 = 25%
10. 0.2727 = 27.27% or 27.3%
11. 0.222 = 22.2%
12. 0.50 = 50%
13. 0.20 = 20%
14. 0.10 = 10%
15. 0.80 = 80%

Practice 32
1. 40/100 = 2/5	16. 9/100
2. 25/100 = 1/4	17. 149/1,000
3. 333/1,000 = 1/3	18. 32/1,000 = 4/125
4. 16/100 = 4/25	19. 44/100 = 11/25
5. 99/100	20. 999/1,000
6. 433/1,000	21. 1/100
7. 18/100 = 9/50	22. 90/100 = 9/10
8. 77/100	23. 65/100 = 13/20
9. 20/100 = 1/5	24. 129/1,000
10. 29/100	25. 11/100
11. 14/100 = 7/50	26. 36/100 = 9/25
12. 169/1,000	27. 199/1,000
13. 6/100 = 3/50	28. 111/1,000
14. 35/100 = 7/20	29. 55/100 = 11/20
15. 135/1,000 = 27/200	30. 707/1,000

Practice 33
1. 4.5	8. 6.4	15. 6
2. 7.2	9. 15.4	16. 54
3. 3.6	10. 282	17. 80
4. 66	11. 25	18. 30
5. 16	12. 2.8	19. 80
6. 5.2	13. 40	20. 240
7. 6.4	14. 50	

Practice 34
1. $6, $24
2. $27, $63
3. $12.50, $37.50
4. $2.50, $22.50
5. $6.90, $39.10
6. $35, $65
7. $14.52, $51.48
8. $7.02, $70.98
9. $2.24, $25.76
10. $96, $224
11. $0.90, $14.10
12. $9.30, $52.70
13. $0.60, $11.40
14. $22, $66
15. $1.40, $12.60
16. $12.40, $49.60

Practice 35
1. Store #1: $14.40, $33.60
   Store #2: $30, $45
   Best deal: Store #1
2. Store #1: $17.60, $62.40
   Store #2: $23.75, $71.25
   Best deal: Store #1
3. Store #1: $23, $77
   Store #2: $8.52, $62.48
   Best deal: Store #2
4. Store #1: $63.90, $149.10
   Store #2: $38, $152
   Best deal: Store #1
5. Store #1: $3.60, $5.40
   Store #2: $9, $6
   Best deal: Store #1
6. Store #1: $0.70, $1.05
   Store #2: $1.44, $0.96
   Best deal: Store #2
7. Store #1: $1.20, $6.80
   Store #2: $2.75, $8.25
   Best deal: Store #1

Practice 36
1. $1,000, $3,000
2. $110, $610
3. $800, $4,800
4. $250, $2,750
5. $10,500, $20,500
6. $1,350, $4,350
7. $1,200, $6,200
8. $264, $1,464
9. $64,000, $104,000
10. $49,500, $104,500

Test Practice 1
1. D	6. A	11. C	16. A
2. C	7. D	12. D	17. B
3. A	8. B	13. C	18. C
4. C	9. D	14. B	19. B
5. B	10. D	15. B	20. D

Test Practice 2
1. C	5. D	9. A	13. C
2. D	6. C	10. A	14. D
3. B	7. B	11. C	15. A
4. D	8. B	12. A	16. A

Test Practice 3
1. B	7. B	13. B	19. B
2. A	8. C	14. B	20. A
3. C	9. C	15. A	21. A
4. A	10. A	16. C	22. C
5. B	11. C	17. C	
6. C	12. D	18. D	

Test Practice 4
1. B	7. C	13. D	19. D
2. C	8. B	14. A	20. D
3. D	9. B	15. D	21. D
4. C	10. D	16. A	22. A
5. C	11. B	17. A	
6. D	12. A	18. A	

Test Practice 5
1. A	7. A	13. D	19. C
2. A	8. D	14. B	20. A
3. C	9. B	15. A	21. A
4. C	10. D	16. C	22. D
5. A	11. A	17. D	
6. B	12. A	18. C	

Test Practice 6
1. A	6. B	11. C	16. B
2. D	7. C	12. A	17. D
3. A	8. A	13. B	18. A
4. B	9. A	14. C	19. D
5. B	10. D	15. B	20. D

©Teacher Created Resources, Inc.